MAKING THE METROPOLIS

· CREATORS OF VICTORIA'S LONDON ·

MAKING THE METROPOLIS
· CREATORS OF VICTORIA'S LONDON ·

STEPHEN HALLIDAY

WITH A FOREWORD BY MAXWELL HUTCHINSON

breedon **books**
PUBLISHING

First published in Great Britain in 2003 by
The Breedon Books Publishing Company Limited
Breedon House, 3 The Parker Centre,
Derby, DE21 4SZ.

ISBN 1 85983 357 8

Printed and bound by Butler & Tanner, Frome, Somerset, England.

Cover printing by Lawrence-Allen Colour Printers, Weston-super-
Mare, Somerset, England.

Contents

Acknowledgements

I have enjoyed writing this book very much. However, much of the price of my doing so has been paid by others. My wife Jane, a midwife; my daughter Faye, a nurse in a busy Accident and Emergency department in Liverpool; and my son Simon, a soldier keeping the peace in the world's troublespots, all have more stressful jobs than I do. Yet they cheerfully endure my frequent absences and listen patiently to my accounts of the colourful people and strange episodes that were involved in the creation of Victorian London. My colleagues Jane Fletcher, Lucia Ingham and Mike Martin, with whom I share responsibility for the management of 160 students, have often helped me by doing parts of my job that I should have been doing myself. The Dean of Buckinghamshire Business School, Nigel Cox, kindly arranges my teaching timetable so that I can have time free from other commitments. In this way I can spend time in the British Library, the Guildhall Library and the Metropolitan Archives doing the research required for a book such as this. Nor would this book have been written without the help of the librarians in those institutions whose legendary patience when dealing with authors is an example to us all. As I write these words I am preparing to attend a retirement lunch for my colleague of many years, Dave Dovey, who has devoted 33 years to instructing our students in the mysteries of English Law. I don't think he'll ever really retire, but I dedicate this book to the memory of those 33 years devoted to the subject he loves and to the benefit of more students than anyone could ever count.

Stephen Halliday
February 2003

Foreword

MOST visitors to London believe they are visiting a truly old city. In some, but not all respects, they are correct. Their preconceptions are fuelled by an overzealous tourist industry which promulgates the idea of an ancient London town.

In fact, they visit and experience very little of genuinely great antiquity. If they are lucky, and well informed, they may see fragments of the 2,000-year-old Roman wall. They are bound to visit the White Tower of London, William the Conqueror's stamp of authority on his newly-won kingdom. Thanks to the Great Fire of 1666 very little of the mediaeval city of London survives (and owing to a similar, but lesser conflagration, Westminster and its associated building, the home of monarchs, met a similar fate). The Guildhall and Westminster Hall show us some of what may have existed without misfortune's flame.

Even Westminster Abbey, founded by Edward the Confessor in 1042 and crowned with the glory of Henry the VII's magnificent perpendicular chapel, is surmounted by twin western towers designed by Nicholas Hawksmoor, built in 1730. In truth, London, as we experience it today, is a 19th-century city. As the pages of this book tell us, London, at the end of the 18th century, consisted of the Square Mile of the City with its mediaeval street pattern and Sir Christopher Wren's baroque churches, a small settlement around the Abbey and Palace of Whitehall, a scattering of country houses, a palace or two, and the original Georgian squares sitting in splendid isolation alongside acres of unkempt marsh land, forest, field and pasture. It took the Victorians, bold as brass in every endeavour, to fashion the world's first true metropolis.

The courage, the daring and the entrepreneurial vision of the engineers, architects and developers featured in these pages reflect the same pioneering spirit as David Livingstone and Cecil Rhodes. A handful of unique, talented and resourceful individuals risked life, fortune and reputation to build the largest city in the world, truly capable of commanding an empire that included a quarter of the world's population.

So much of what we take for granted in the London of today was quickly, earnestly and expeditiously wrought during the 19th century. John Nash carved thoroughfares and circuses and built terraces fit for the Empress of India; the Brunels, father and son, made deep tunnelling possible, without which Sir Edward Watkin's Metropolitan

A handful of unique, talented and resourceful individuals risked life, fortune and reputation to build the largest city in the world

Railway and the subsequent tube system would have been unachievable; Thomas Cubitt was not daunted by the task of developing acre upon acre of what is now considered to be some of the most elegant urban housing in the world. Joseph Paxton and Alfred Waterhouse changed the perception of architectural structure, form and ornament and Joseph Bazalgette must still be remembered every time we flush the WC.

Joseph Bazalgette must still be remembered every time we flush the WC

Those responsible for London since World War Two have precious little to show for the privilege of ownership and custodianship of this truly great city. On the contrary, since the Festival of Britain of 1951 (enthusiastically conjured up 100 years after the Great Exhibition, during the post-war years of severe privation and austerity), the story has been one of complacency, neglect and accelerating decay.

The tube system, in the tunnels made possible by the pioneering work of Marc Brunel, is in a seemingly eternal state of decline. The ageing Victorian railway system has been mortgaged to the private sector, which seems to lack even the financial acumen of the impecunious and fumbling John Nash. The M25 orbital road was so ill conceived and executed that it does not deserve the title 'motorway', for making a clear way for the motor is the last thing it does. In contrast, Bazalgette's Victorian sewer system is still man enough for our increasing amounts of water-borne waste.

At least Croydon, Manchester and Sheffield have their cost-effective tram systems, while London still manages with many of its 50-year-old Routemaster omnibuses.

Those responsible for the London of the third millennium lack the foresight, energy and entrepreneurial zeal, skill and enthusiasm of those who built the city that we enjoy today. The Mayor of London and the members of the Greater London Authority should keep a copy of this book beside their beds.

I am proud to say that London is now my subject. Despite that, my day-to-day enjoyment of my chosen home town has been greatly enhanced by the history in this book. Cities are living stories, but to read and understand them we have to know their language – once we do, every step, corner, pavement, building, statue and structure becomes a daily joy.

The Victorians who are the subject of this book made sense and order out of a mushrooming metropolis, and Stephen Halliday has made sense and order out of the complex history of what is, arguably, still the greatest city on Earth.

Maxwell Hutchinson
London 2003

PROLOGUE

The World City

I N 1801, the date of the first census, the population of London was 959,000 – already the world's largest city. When Victoria took the throne in 1837 the population was approaching two million. At her death in 1901 it had passed six and a half million. This book is an account of the engineers, architects, builders and businessmen who created Victoria's metropolis. They built the dwellings which housed the city's aristocrats and artisans. They designed and constructed the infrastructure which made the city work and which made it safe: the streets, the tunnels, the railways, the river crossings and the sewers which banished the waterborne diseases that plagued Victorian cities. They designed its great public and monumental buildings like the Houses of Parliament and the museums.

They knew one another. Some were friends, some colleagues and some were rivals. Some of them were given the task of rectifying the mistakes of the others. **John Nash** (1752–1835) created the 'royal mile' from Regent's Park to St James's Park, but left Buckingham Palace an uninhabitable ruin faced by an incongruous and impassable monolith called the 'Marble Arch'. **Thomas Cubitt** (1788–1855) made Buckingham Palace a home fit for a queen and found a permanent home for Nash's arch. He also turned Belgravia from a foetid swamp into a home for the aristocracy while creating Bloomsbury and Pimlico for the aspiring middle classes. He was, moreover, one of the early advocates of the Great Exhibition of 1851, whose Crystal Palace was designed by **Sir Joseph Paxton** (1803–65), and Cubitt later negotiated the purchase of land for the site of the Kensington museums, using the profits of the Great Exhibition to pay for it. **Alfred Waterhouse** (1830–1905) designed the first of those museums to be built – the Natural History Museum. **Sir Charles Barry** (1795–1860) designed one of London's most famous buildings, the New Palace of Westminster, after the old palace was burned down in 1834. Its position on the banks of the Thames exposed its occupants to the full force of the 'Great Stink' of 1858 – a crisis for which **Sir Joseph Bazalgette** (1819–1891) was prepared. Bazalgette designed and constructed the system of drains, sewers, pumping stations and treatment works which turned the Thames from a stinking, cholera-

Buckingham Palace an uninhabitable ruin faced by an incongruous and impassable monolith called the 'Marble Arch'.

9

infested hazard into a clean river. He also built famous streets, bridges and parks. He proposed a new bridge between the Tower of London and the south bank. This, London's most famous bridge, was eventually built, though not to Bazalgette's design. The engineer for Tower Bridge was Charles Barry's son, Sir John Wolfe-Barry (1836–1918).

Others were also creating structures which, though less visible, were essential to the comfort of London's citizens. **Marc Brunel's** (1769–1849) invention of the tunnelling shield led not only to the construction of the world's first tunnel beneath a river, but also made possible the creation of London's tube railways. Marc's son Isambard Kingdom Brunel (1806–59) acknowledged the superiority of Joseph Paxton's Crystal Palace over his own design for the Great Exhibition and was later inspired by Paxton's use of glass in his plan for Paddington Station. Marc's grandson, Henry Brunel, son of Isambard, helped Sir John Wolfe-Barry with the design of Tower Bridge. **Sir Edward Watkin** (1819–1901) used Brunel's tunnel for his East London Railway and also became the chairman of the world's first underground railway, the Metropolitan. This in turn created 'Metroland', the middle-class suburban landscape which was celebrated in Betjeman's verse.

In 1801 London was a disparate collection of ramshackle communities mostly run by vestrymen. By the time of Victoria's death in 1901 it was the world's first metropolis, the heart of the greatest empire the world had ever seen, from which her successor, Edward VII, ruled over a quarter of the world's population. This book is the account of that transformation and the men who achieved it. Each of them deserves his turn on that vacant plinth in Trafalgar Square which has long exercised the minds of the great and the good.

In 1801 London was a disparate collection of ramshackle communities mostly run by vestrymen

CHAPTER 1

John Nash and Regency London

As a speculative builder, this gentleman amassed a large fortune.
(*Annual Register*, 1835, obituary of John Nash)

Look at the manner in which the interior of St James's Park was, in a few months, converted from a swampy meadow into a luxurious garden, and then let the reader ask himself whether the metropolis is or is not indebted to the traduced object of this notice.
(*John Bull* obituary of John Nash)

... the most inspired planner that London has known.
(Pevsner's *Buildings of England, Cities of London and Westminster*, Penguin, 1978, page 87)

John Nash. (By courtesy of the National Portrait Gallery, London)

JOHN NASH (1752–1835) is remembered principally as the architect of Brighton Pavilion and the creator of Regent Street. It is not clear that he should be regarded as an architect at all. He described himself as a carpenter and most of his work would classify him as an urban planner (a discipline then unrecognised) or a speculative builder. In connection with the latter activity he has acquired a slightly shady reputation for murky financial dealings. If there is any truth at all in this charge then he must be adjudged a failure in the matter since he died penniless, having sunk most of his money in the great London building projects which are his memorial. He was certainly well-connected. The Prince Regent, later George IV, was his greatest, and certainly his most extravagant, patron. He was also a close friend of the artist J.M.W. Turner, who painted for Nash two pictures of Nash's house on the Isle of Wight. These are now in the Tate Gallery.

John Nash was born in 1752, probably in Lambeth, though a claim has also been entered for Cardigan, in Wales, the ancestral home of his mother. His father was a millwright – a profession which demanded much skill and which produced many self-taught engineers. In 1767 John Nash was articled to the well-known architect Robert Taylor, who had designed the Stone Buildings, Lincoln's Inn, and had been one of the original governors of Thomas Coram's Foundling Hospital, which he had helped to design. In 1778 John Nash's uncle Thomas died. Thomas, his father's brother, had owned and managed a calico printing works close to the present site of the Royal Festival Hall and made a great fortune, £1,000 of which he left to his nephew. Thomas was buried in a fine mausoleum in Kent which he had commissioned for himself and in whose design John Nash may have played some part.

The Prince Regent was his greatest, and certainly his most extravagant, patron

Speculative building

For the next six years Nash, describing himself as a carpenter, became a speculative builder, constructing and sometimes converting properties which he purchased in London. In 1782 he acquired a terrace of houses on Great Russell Street between Bury Place and Bloomsbury Square, added some Corinthian columns and stucco to the brick façade and adopted three of the houses as his residence[1]. This was Nash's first use of 'Parker's stucco', a material with which his buildings were to become most strongly associated. It had become viable as a building material as a result of improvements in the manufacture of cement by a man called Parker in the 1780s. His association with stucco, later adopted by many builders, attracted satirists as stuccoed buildings mushroomed throughout Nash's later developments. It was even celebrated in verse:

> *Augustus at Rome was for building renowned,*
> *For of marble he left what of brick he had found;*
> *But is not our Nash, too, a very great master?*
> *He finds us all brick and he leaves us all plaster.*[2]

Nash's enterprise was not a success. In October, 1783, his bankruptcy was announced in the *London Gazette* and he left London for Carmarthenshire, close to his mother's family home. For the next 12 years he rebuilt his reputation and his finances by undertaking a series of less risky, if more prosaic, projects. He designed three prisons in Carmarthen, Cardigan and Hereford, following the specifications of the great prison reformer John Howard, all of which survived into the 20th century. It was during this provincial period of his practice that he hired as a draughtsman a penniless émigré Frenchman called Auguste de Pugin, father of the architect Augustus Welby Pugin (1812–52), who was responsible for the ornamentation of the rebuilt Houses of Parliament.

Return to London

In 1796, his fortunes restored, Nash returned to London and opened a practice which involved designing and building country houses in England, Scotland, Wales and Ireland. The work involved much travel. He told the diarist Joseph Farington that at this time he had 'travelled in the three Kingdoms Eleven thousand miles in the year and in that time he had expended £1,500 in chaise hire'.[3] He also took as articled pupils two of the sons of Sir Humphrey Repton (1752–1818), who was already very well established as a landscape gardener. It is not known how Nash came to be acquainted with Repton but it may have been through Repton's contacts that Nash gained many of his country house commissions. The two were certainly closely associated for the period 1796 to 1800. Again it may have been through Repton that Nash came to design a conservatory for the Prince of Wales, a drawing of which he exhibited at the Royal Academy in 1798. Over the next three years Nash was paid £264 and sixpence from the privy purse for commissions he undertook for the Prince.

In December 1798 Nash married Mary Bradley, the daughter of a not particularly prosperous coal merchant. At this time Nash became wealthy. He bought a fine house at 28–9 Dover Street in the fashionable heart of Mayfair. Nash also built himself a country home called East Cowes Castle on the Isle of Wight and two other properties on the island, one of which was occupied over the next few years by five children called Pennethorne who were supposedly distant relatives of the new Mrs Nash. There has been some speculation about the source of his new-found prosperity. It may be that he was spending the commissions he had been earning for his 10 years of work on country houses. It has also been suggested that the wealth was brought to the marriage by Mary and originated with the Prince of Wales, whose mistress, according to some accounts, she had been. Some have even suggested that the Prince was the father of the children and Mary Nash the mother. No evidence has been produced for either the sudden wealth or the exotic explanations, but a royal connection would explain how it was that, in 1806, Nash was appointed architect to the

'travelled in the three Kingdoms Eleven thousand miles in the year and in that time he had expended £1,500 in chaise hire'

Chief Commissioner of Woods and Forests. This was not a well-paid post, but it was coveted since the holder was, in effect, chief architect to the Government. He had access to influential figures in the Government and was well placed to gain access to contracts for designing and constructing Crown properties.

Marylebone Park

It was in his capacity as architect to the Commissioner that Nash became associated with the project with which he is most often connected. In 1794 a Scotsman called John Fordyce had been appointed to the post of Surveyor-General of His Majesty's Land Revenue, in which capacity he was responsible for all Crown lands. He proposed that a map be made of all the Crown's estates in London, since some confusion existed over questions of ownership and boundaries. His attention was drawn to Marylebone Park, an area which had been a royal hunting ground in the time of the early Stuarts. In 1794 the park was used as a dairy farm, supplying milk, butter and cream to the London markets. It was held under a lease by the Duke of Portland, owner of nearby Portland Place, but the lease was due to expire in 1811, at which time the park would revert to the Crown. It was on the northern edge of the built-up area of London at that time and Fordyce recommended that a plan be drawn up to develop the area. The task was awarded to Nash in his official capacity.

A Nash villa in Regent's Park, 2002.

Fordyce died in 1810 before the lease expired and Nash submitted his first proposal[4] to the Prime Minister, Spencer Perceval. Perceval was shortly to achieve the unenviable distinction of being assassinated in that office. Nash's first plan, prepared in competition with others, envisaged a rather grand housing estate, with terraces of fine houses stretching around the periphery of the park and 26 fine villas within the park itself. Perceval wanted fewer houses and more park, so Nash prepared a new design, incorporating only eight villas within the park. This was essentially the plan which was eventually adopted. Plans for two terraces to the north were abandoned, the space being occupied instead, from 1827, by the London Zoo. The Commissioners were particularly impressed by the prospects of increased Crown revenue that Nash's plan envisaged. Rents of £54,429 were predicted in return for an investment of £12,115, though, like most of Nash's financial predictions, this was wildly optimistic. The Commissioners' enthusiasm is not entirely concealed by their portentous language:

'... *although Mr Nash had considered beauty and ornament to a very considerable degree, he had still made it a principal object of his attention to form a Plan with a view to a very great increase of Revenue*'.[5]

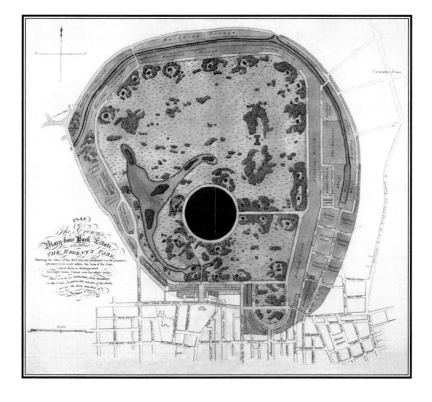

Plan of Regent's Park showing the sites for 26 villas to be built within the park's area and some surrounding streets, 1822. (By courtesy of the Guildhall Library, Corporation of London)

The terraces around the park were named after the titles held by the Prince Regent or his brothers, but Nash added new features including a lake. He alighted upon an existing plan, promoted by a man called Thomas Homer, to extend the Grand Junction Canal[6] from Paddington basin to Limehouse, where access could be gained to the expanding London docks. If the canal could be routed through the park then it would provide a ready source of water for the lake that Nash had now incorporated in his design. Moreover, by constructing a canal basin within the park produce could be brought from the countryside to the market that Nash wanted to create for the convenience of residents. He explained that 'many Persons would consider the circumstances of Boats and Barges passing along the Canal as enlivening the scenery, provided the Bargemen or People from the Boats were prevented from landing in the Parks'. This argument did not find favour. Bargemen were a notoriously rough bunch and the Commissioners were concerned that the wealthy inhabitants whom they hoped to tempt to buy dwellings in the park would be alarmed at the prospect of having their tranquillity disturbed by bargemen's oaths, and worse. Accordingly the canal was routed round the northern periphery of the park where it remains, the Regent's Canal. A basin was constructed within the park for the projected market and this remained until it was filled in during World War Two. In order to promote the venture Nash bought £15,000 of shares in the canal. It was one of his many unwise investments. Construction began after the necessary Act had been passed in 1812 and was completed in 1820 after many vicissitudes caused by the original promoter, Thomas Homer, who had embezzled much of the capital. Nash had to wait until 1829 for the first, modest dividend of 12 shillings and sixpence on each £100 of capital.

Nash was sure that 'the attraction of open space, free air and the scenery of nature' on the edge of the capital would attract residents of the highest quality, and for this reason he inveighed against the use of speculative builders who, he suggested, would build shoddy houses.[7]

the wealthy inhabitants whom they hoped to tempt to buy dwellings in the park would be alarmed at the prospect of having their tranquillity disturbed by bargemen's oaths

> 'it is in the interest of those concerned in such building that they should be of as little cost as possible, preserving an attractive exterior which Parker's stucco, coloured bricks and balconies accomplish ... a very few years will exhibit cracked walls, swagged floors, bulged fronts, crooked roofs, leaky gutters, inadequate drains and other ills of an originally bad constitution'.

Presumably he excluded his own speculative building activities from these strictures, particularly since he was already becoming strongly associated with the despised 'Parker's stucco'.

One of Fordyce's recommendations had been the construction of a new street from Marylebone to Westminster. At the time that Nash was drawing up his plans there was a marked contrast between the wide streets and spacious squares of Mayfair, to the north of Piccadilly, and the narrow streets and tenements of Soho, further to the east. The 'May Fair' had been transferred in 1688 from the Haymarket to the present site of Shepherd Market. In the 18th century the area was developed by the Grosvenor family, later dukes of Westminster and patrons of Thomas Cubitt.[8] Mayfair's wide avenues and spacious squares attracted wealthy aristocrats whose names are still commemorated in thoroughfares like Devonshire Street and Chesterfield Gardens, long after the stately homes they once accommodated have passed away. Only Burlington House remains, as the home of the Royal Academy. In 1764 the fair itself was suppressed at the request of the residents, but the name remained. The neighbouring district of Soho had developed a very different character. In 1536 the convent and leper hospital which owned St Giles's Field, as the area was known, had surrendered the land to Henry VIII upon the dissolution of the religious houses. It had then been used as a royal park in which the king could hunt while resident at Whitehall Palace. The name 'Soho' which it acquired at this time was a hunting cry. In the late 17th century French Huguenots[9] moved into the area, fleeing from the persecutions of Louis XIV. Soho Square retains its French church to this day. In 1739 the chronicler William Maitland wrote of Soho that 'It is an easy matter for a Stranger to imagine himself in France', many of the immigrants being very poor. The area thus began an association with foreign residents that it has never lost. By Nash's time the great aristocratic houses like Leicester House had been abandoned and Leicester Square itself was derelict, remaining so until it was reconstructed at the expense of Albert Grant's unfortunate investors.[10]

The name 'Soho' which it acquired at this time was a hunting cry.

The 'New Street'

In 1813 Parliament passed 'An Act for making a more convenient Communication from Marylebone Park to Charing Cross', commonly known as the 'New Street Act'. Nash proposed a route which 'should cross the eastern entrance to all the Streets occupied by the higher classes and to leave to the east all the bad streets'.[11] It would thus form a *cordon sanitaire* between the two areas: in his words 'a Line of Separation between the habitations of the first class of Society and those of the inferior classes ... mechanics and the trading part of the community'.[12] It would also provide a suitably magnificent route, a 'Royal Mile', between the Prince Regent's projected summer palace in Marylebone Park (soon to be renamed Regent's Park) and his London residence, Carlton House, overlooking the Mall and St James's Park. In the event Carlton House was abandoned and demolished when the Prince grew tired of it and the idea of the summer palace died with the Prince himself in 1830.

The road would begin in the park itself. Its first obstacle was the 'New Road' which had been built in 1756 to connect the village of Paddington, on the edge of Westminster, with the Angel on the edge of the City. The New Road is now Marylebone Road–Euston Road–Pentonville Road. It was proposed to create a huge 'circus' to effect this crossing. In the event only the southern side of the circus was built and this now forms Park Crescent. From there the road would run south along what became Portland Place, Langham Place, and the road soon to be named 'Regent Street', which turned east as it approached Piccadilly in order to avoid the fashionable and royal area of St James. The easterly turn would be executed by means of a curve that became known as 'the Quadrant', which would be occupied, according to Nash's plan, by 'shops appropriated to articles of fashion and taste' for the aristocracy. Regent Street would cross Piccadilly via another circus, soon known as Piccadilly Circus. On the site later

1836 view of Regent Street Quadrant, looking north, showing the colonnades which were demolished and embarrassingly auctioned in 1848. (By courtesy of the Guildhall Library, Corporation of London)

occupied by Eros it was proposed to erect a temple to Shakespeare in the Doric style. Regent Street would then cross Pall Mall.

Pall Mall owed its name to the fact that, at the time of Charles II, the area had accommodated a royal *Palla a Maglio*[13] alley – a game rather like croquet which was much favoured by the King, who was living at St James's nearby. The area's association with royalty made it extremely fashionable. Mrs Maria Fitzherbert, the Prince Regent's unacknowledged wife, lived in Pall Mall from 1789–96. According to Nash's proposals Pall Mall would be widened to give access to another 'circus' to the east, which, Nash proposed, would become a home for learned societies like the Royal Academy and the Royal Society, with the National Gallery on the north side. This circus later became Trafalgar Square and gave access to Whitehall and the Houses of Parliament further to the south. Having crossed Pall Mall, Regent Street would terminate at Carlton House, the Prince's London home. This had been rebuilt between 1783 and 1813, at enormous public expense, only to be abandoned by the Prince when he became king. It was demolished in 1827, an act described by his biographer as 'the one truly wicked act George IV committed'.[14] Many of the fireplaces and furnishings were removed to Windsor and Buckingham Palace, while the Corinthian columns were later used to support the portico of the National Gallery in Trafalgar Square. The house was replaced by

View of Regent Street, Westminster, looking towards the Duke of York's Column, depicting what is now Piccadilly Circus, 1842. (By courtesy of the Guildhall Library, Corporation of London)

'the one truly wicked act George IV committed'

View of Trafalgar Square, Westminster, as planned by Nash, showing the design for a building to house the Royal Academy of Arts with King's Mews in the distance. (By courtesy of the Guildhall Library, Corporation of London)

Carlton House Terrace, to Nash's design, which remains as an example of Nash's finest work. Moreover, it attracted tenants of such varying distinction as William Gladstone, Lords Palmerston and Curzon, Earl Grey and Joachim von Ribbentrop, Adolf Hitler's ambassador.

Building the 'New Street'

Nash now began to negotiate with the owners of property along the route. Seven hundred houses were demolished, but since these were mostly on the 'Soho' part of the route and occupied by 'mechanics and the trading part of the community' they did not create too many

View looking south from Waterloo Place showing Nash's Carlton House Terrace and Duke of York's Column, with a group of people wearing the latest winter fashions for 1837 and 1838 standing in the foreground. (By courtesy of the Guildhall Library, Corporation of London)

problems. Others were better connected and more obdurate. One of these was Sir James Langham. In 1767 Lord Foley had built a mansion at the southern end of the Duke of Portland's estate, having first secured from the Duke a guarantee that no building would ever obscure Foley's view northwards towards Hampstead and Highgate. This is the reason that Portland Place, which lay in front of Foley's house, is one of the widest streets in London. It had been laid out in 1778 by the Adam brothers with a width of 125 feet, the same as Foley's house. In 1814 Nash acquired the Foley estate in settlement of a debt and sold part of it to Sir James Langham.

Langham was obliged by Nash to buy more land than he really needed for his house because Nash threatened to run the new street uncomfortably close to the front windows of the house. He has given his name to Langham Place and the Langham Hotel, the latter occupying the site of his former home.

In the years that followed, Nash devoted much of his time and some of his money to the New Street and the areas that it connected. He chose a Palladian style of architecture – a more restrained version of the Baroque which had prevailed earlier in the 18th century. His task was to lay out the plans and elevations of the streets and terraces, while leaving the detailed design to builders to whom the individual plots were sold. In return the builders paid fees to Nash for his preliminary work. When a Select Committee asked him in 1828 'How are you remunerated for your trouble in giving elevations and general plans of these new streets?' Nash replied 'Very badly' and explained the procedure:[15]

View of Foley House in 1796. The house's frontage determined the generous width of Portland Place. (By courtesy of the Guildhall Library, Corporation of London)

View along Portland Place, 1831, towards Regent's Park. The street owes its generous proportions to the width of Foley House. (By courtesy of the Guildhall Library, Corporation of London)

'I negotiate the original purchase of the ground, negotiate the letting of the ground, make the designs for the elevations; I set out the ground for the building, draw up the terms of building; I superintend it in a general way in the execution; I draw the plans on the leases; for all of which I receive a fee of one half year's ground rent.'

This payment could amount to £10 for one lease. In many cases Nash himself did more detailed design work for the buildings, handing rough sketches to his draughtsmen, who turned them into working drawings for builders. The builders might then make their own alterations as they went along and Nash whose 'general way' of superintendence was often very accommodating, either didn't notice or didn't mind, his main concern being to maintain steady progress on the development. In this way the terraces surrounding Regent's Park itself, including York Terrace, Cumberland Terrace, Chester Terrace and Cambridge Terrace were designed, as was Park Crescent, to the south of New Road (Marylebone Road). At 152–4 Albany Street, on the eastern edge of the park, Nash designed a military hospital to specialise in the treatment of eye injuries. It later became the London home of the inventor Goldsworthy Gurney (1793–1875), where Gurney invented the blowtorch, limelight and a steam-powered car, in which he travelled from London to Bath at an average speed of 15 miles per hour. He was just the sort of resident whom Nash, and no doubt the Prince Regent, wanted to attract to the new development. Others followed, including the French and American ambassadors, Joseph Bonaparte, Lord Lister, (father of antiseptic surgery) and Wilkie Collins. The area is rich in blue plaques.

a steam-powered car, in which he travelled from London to Bath at an average speed of 15 miles per hour

All Souls' Church

At the bottom of Portland Place the new street had to execute a sharp double bend in order to avoid James Langham's home before proceeding south into Regent Street itself. In order to conceal the awkwardness of the bend Nash designed a church to occupy the junction: All Souls' Langham Place, now situated immediately outside the headquarters of the BBC. All Souls' is the only surviving church built by Nash. Its design, with a Gothic spire on a classical rotunda, attracted much criticism. In a debate in the House of Commons one MP asked for:[16]

'... the name of the architect under whose directions the new church in Langham Place is constructing. Everybody who saw it shrugged up their shoulders and inquired who

could be the architect who invented such a monstrosity ... He should like also to hear what this mass of deformity had cost ... though he was not rich he was not unwilling to contribute a fair proportion of the expense ... of pulling it down'.

Another was reported in *The Observer* as offering 'a trifle to have this church pulled down'.[17] The Commissioner of Woods and Forests admitted, reluctantly, that the architect was 'an obscure individual named Nash' and a few days later a cartoon appeared of Nash, most uncomfortably impaled on the spire of the church, with the caption 'Nashional Taste'. Perhaps it is not surprising that Nash seems to have lost patience with his critics after designing the rotunda and is reported to have exclaimed 'I've had enough of this now. Stick a big box on the back for the rest of the church. I'm off down the pub'![18] The church was completed in 1824.

Regent Street

Regent Street itself attracted a variety of developments including a hotel, a bank and the church commissioners, who were anxious to ensure that the spiritual needs of the new inhabitants would be adequately served. It would also have shops and galleries at ground level with residences above them. Much of Regent Street was financed by loans that Nash made to builders from his ever-diminishing fortune. This was a device that Nash used particularly in the Quadrant, where he wanted to exercise sufficient control over the development to ensure a degree of stylistic uniformity. The 'shops appropriated to articles of fashion and taste' which Nash prescribed for the Quadrant would be fronted by a colonnade to shelter from the rain the men and women of fashion who, it was confidently anticipated, would wish to promenade along the new street. Referring to such people Nash wrote:

'Nashional taste!!!'; showing John Nash spiked by the seat of his trousers on the spire of All Souls', Langham Place, 1824. (By courtesy of the Guildhall Library, Corporation of London)

'those who have nothing to do but walk about and amuse themselves may do so every day in the week, instead of being frequently confined many days together to their houses by rain ... the occupiers of the Lodgings can see and converse with those passing in the Carriages underneath, which will add to the gaiety of the scene and induce single men, and others, who only visit Town occasionally, to give a preference to such Lodgings'.[19]

In 1821 a contemporary diarist, Joseph Farington, who knew and visited Nash, reported that: 'John Nash, the architect, was at a stand in money matters – that he owed £800,000 if not a million'[20] This was certainly an exaggeration. Debts on this scale were run up only by Nash's royal patron and the architect's debts were discharged quite soon after his death, but Farington's report of this contemporary rumour does reflect the strain that the development imposed on his finances. The Commissioners were also disappointed with the returns on their investment, which did not approach the extravagant levels predicted by Nash in his original plan.[21] Nash informed them, rather late in the day, 'I always looked to a remote period for a full consummation of the hopes I held out as to Revenue'[22]

In Lower Regent Street, beyond its junction with Carlton Street, Nash built a mansion for himself. On the first floor was a fine picture gallery which contained copies of Raphael's works in the Vatican, executed by an English painter, with the permission of the Pope, at a cost to Nash of £3,000. The gallery was later dismantled and re-erected in Nash's home at East Cowes on the Isle of Wight. In 1848 the colonnades were also removed from the Quadrant, having failed to attract an adequate number of fashionable promenaders. Shopkeepers complained that the colonnades darkened their windows. They were auctioned in a rather jocular spirit according to *The Builder*, most of those attending the auction being:

> '*brokers and dealers chiefly; some of whom, with little respect for poor Nash, declared that the very handsome columns were excellently good for a workhouse, while others talked good humouredly about chimney ornaments.*'

The auctioneer began the proceedings by proposing an opening bid of £10, but was forced to retreat to £7 10s, at which price he sold a few, the others remaining on his hands. Their original cost was £35.[23] These were not the last indignities that Nash's work had to suffer. By the late 19th century the shops that Nash had thought worthy of the New Street and its aristocratic visitors were no longer profitable. One shopkeeper lamented that he was now having to deal with the middle classes, at lower profit margins, and that a much greater turnover was required than could be achieved in the boutiques that Nash had designed for the street. In the 1920s virtually all of Nash's buildings north of Piccadilly were redeveloped and all we have to remember him by is the elegant curve of the Quadrant as it turns into Piccadilly Circus. In Lower Regent Street his designs for the Haymarket Theatre,

'John Nash, the architect, was at a stand in money matters – that he owed £800,000 if not a million'[20]

the United Services Club and Carlton House Terrace do survive, the last of these providing a home for the Royal Society, which Nash himself had proposed for nearby Trafalgar Square. The Athenaeum, nearby, was designed by Decimus Burton, one of Nash's associates in the development of Regent Street, and built between 1828 and 1830.

By Royal Command

In 1821, as the Regent Street development proceeded, Nash was drawn into the plans for creating a suitably resplendent London home for his royal patron, now, at last, George IV. It was through this connection that Nash now earned a reputation for extravagance in the use of public money – perhaps an inevitable result of his association with the new king. Nash had long been George's favourite architect. George even tried to use Nash's services in a more delicate capacity in negotiations with the Government over the his troubled relationship with Queen Caroline. The Government, in the person of Nash's friend Sir Samuel Romilly, Solicitor General,

View of Nash's Haymarket Theatre, 1840. (By courtesy of the Guildhall Library, Corporation of London)

DECIMUS BURTON (1800–81)

Decimus Burton was associated with John Nash in designing many of the buildings to accompany Nash's developments in London, and also rivalled Sir Joseph Paxton in his pioneering use of glass. He laid out the grounds of London Zoo on the north side of Regent's Park. Much of his work has been replaced, but his giraffe house remains in use for its original purpose, together with a raven's aviary and clock tower. He laid out Hyde Park and designed the palm house and temperate house at Kew Gardens, the triumphal arch at Hyde Park Corner and the Athenaeum in Nash's Waterloo Place. The palm house at Kew was inspired by Paxton's 'Great Stove' and itself preceded the even more dramatic use of glass by Paxton in his Crystal Palace.

rejected the architect's clumsy attempt to influence them in the King's favour, but the episode illustrates the King's trust in Nash as well as his ingenuousness.

Nash had already been involved in some of the king's building projects. In 1812 he had been asked to convert a ranger's cottage in Windsor Great Park into a suitable country residence for the Prince. Nash's original estimate for the work was £2,750, but the involvement of the Prince ensured that the cost soon grew to £17,000, and by 1814 it had reached £52,000. It became known as Royal Lodge and was one of the Prince's favourite residences. In the 20th century, much altered, it became the home of Her Majesty Queen Elizabeth the Queen Mother, as did Clarence House, another of Nash's designs that was much altered in subsequent centuries. In 1813 Nash had added a Gothic dining room to the already magnificent Carlton House and the following year he organised a spectacle in St James's Park. The park had long been an unattractive swamp and Nash was engaged on designing the park as we now know it when he was asked to organise an entertainment for some distinguished visitors. This involved building a Chinese bridge, surmounted by a pagoda, to cross the new lake, and an accompanying firework display. The fireworks set fire to the pagoda, resulting in a conflagration which must have exceeded even the Prince's expectations. This was the sort of architect that the Prince liked, so in 1814 he asked Nash to take over from Henry Holland the task of creating Brighton Pavilion. This had originally been a modest farmhouse belonging to the developer Thomas Kemp, creator of Kemptown, and had been purchased in 1787. Holland had been at work on it for over 20 years, but his restrained, tasteful neo-classical villa had failed impress the Prince as being suitably grand, so Nash was appointed in his place. At the enormous cost of £160,000 Nash created, in 1822, the extravagant domed fantasy which was more to the Prince's taste.

The fireworks set fire to the pagoda, resulting in a conflagration which must have exceeded even the Prince's expectations.

'The king's house in Pimlico'

Buckingham House, originally the home of the dukes of Buckingham, had been purchased by George III in 1762 as a residence for his mother and had become known as 'the king's house, Pimlico'. Having decided that the magnificent Carlton House, which some commentators compared favourably with Versailles, was 'antiquated, run down and decrepit', George persuaded the Government to allocate the 'utmost sum' of £350,000 to the transformation of Buckingham House into a palace suitably resplendent for so grand a monarch as George IV. The task had originally been given to Sir John Soane (1753–1837), architect of the new Bank of England, but, given Nash's record at the Royal Lodge and Brighton Pavilion, it was not surprising that, in 1821, Soane was told to pass over the existing plans to the King's favourite architect. Soane was not pleased and was probably not consoled when he received the following letter as 'consolation' from Nash, with its sardonic references to Soane's Masonic connections (which he shared with the King):

> 'Brother Soane,
> You was in a miff when I saw you at the head of your
> Masons. One of the Masonic rules, I am told, is to acquire
> a meek and humble spirit. I fear therefore that you are not
> qualified for Grand Master.'[24]

SIR JOHN SOANE (1753–1837)

Sir John Soane, the son of a bricklayer, trained at the Royal Academy schools from 1771. He later travelled in Italy and became professor of architecture at the Royal Academy in 1809. As surveyor (architect) to the Bank of England from 1788 he exercised much influence upon the design of public buildings in England in the early 19th century. His most visible monument is his design for the Bank of England as we now know it. He also designed Dulwich Picture Gallery. He adopted the practice of opening his house and library in Lincoln's Inn Fields to students of the Royal Academy on the days before and after his lectures. In 1831 he was knighted, supposedly declining a baronetcy in order to prevent his undeserving son from inheriting the title. In 1833 he obtained an Act of Parliament by which his house became Sir John Soane's Museum. It remains a museum of architecture which is open to the public free of charge. (Telephone 0207 440 4263).

Nash's design involved adding two wings to the existing terraced structure, creating a shallow 'U' with the open end of the 'U' pointing towards the Mall. At the entrance would be a huge triumphal arch in marble through which the royal carriage would pass into the open courtyard. The original terrace would be surmounted by a dome. The costs rose more rapidly than the building. Far from the 'utmost sum' of £350,000 proving sufficient, £500,000 was quickly passed. Nash was summoned before a parliamentary committee to defend both his design and its ever-growing cost.[25] Particular attention was focussed upon the dome, which was variously described as 'an inverted egg cup' and 'a common slop pail turned upside down'. As far as the committee

*'a common slop
pail turned upside
down'*

members could ascertain the dome served no useful purpose while involving needless expense

In explanation of the escalating cost Nash told the Committee that 'whenever I saw him [the King] it generally happened that he ordered some alteration'. He further explained that all the merchants in London had been unable to supply the quantity of marble required for his arch, so he had sent an agent to Italy to deal directly with the owners of the Carrara quarries. The arch now stood, incongruous and isolated, at the end of the Mall. It now supplanted the dome as the most mocked feature of the palace and was the subject of a ribald cartoon by William Heath in 1829 featuring 'John Bull and the ARCH – itect WOT builds the arches'. The Chancellor of the Exchequer, Henry Goulburn, instructed Nash that he was to make no more alterations to the design without the permission of the Treasury and when the Prime Minister, the Duke of Wellington, was approached by Nash with some proposed alterations he replied 'If you expect me to put my hand to any additional expense, I'll be damned if I will.' Nash was now, in 1829, in the unhappy position of trying to satisfy a king who continued to demand alterations and a Government which would refuse to pay for them.

'An appropriate emblem for the triumphal arch of the new palace – dedicated to the poor pennyless-priest-ridden and paralysed John Bull'; showing John Bull in fool's cap standing on top of Marble Arch with the new Buckingham Palace behind, 1829. The satire is an attack on the extravagant expenditure on the new palace. (By courtesy of the Guildhall Library, Corporation of London)

The dilemma was resolved when the King died in June 1830. Shortly afterwards Nash, now 78 years old, had a stroke and had little more to do with the palace. By that time the cost had reached £600,000, leaving the palace an uninhabitable wreck with doors that didn't close and drains and lavatories that didn't work. The king had recommended a baronetcy for his faithful architect but Wellington demurred, suggesting that such an honour was inappropriate while the problems associated with Nash's work on the palace remained unresolved. The task was handed to another architect, Edward Blore, and another builder, Thomas Cubitt, in another reign, and was completed at a fraction of the cost that Nash and the Prince would have incurred. The marble arch was found to be too narrow to accommodate state carriages so in 1850 it was dismantled by Thomas Cubitt and the pieces temporarily stored in St James's Park. In 1851 they were re-assembled by Cubitt at the top of Park Lane and given the name Marble Arch.[26]

The various commissions of enquiry which had investigated the public projects in which Nash was involved were relatively kind to him. The 'Select Committee appointed to inquire into the conduct of Mr Nash' concluded that 'No Evidence has been laid before the

Committee to justify any charge of fraud against Mr Nash'[27]. However, an MP called Davies probably reflected public exasperation more faithfully when he told the House of Commons in May 1829 that 'the charge that he had to make against Mr Nash was one of gross and direct fraud on the public'.[28] Another MP called Baring was probably closer to the mark when he observed that:

> '... from what he had heard of Mr Nash he should be inclined to think that he was incapable of dishonesty; but he must say that, as a manager of the public money and as an exhibitor of taste he was sorry the public ever had anything to do with him'.

At the time of George IV's death Nash was 77 years old and his career was virtually at an end. He supervised the construction of Carlton House Terrace, which was completed in 1832, and submitted a design for the National Gallery, which was to be built on the north side of his planned square (Trafalgar Square), although another design was preferred. He died on 18 May 1835, and was buried in the graveyard of the church at East Cowes, close to his home at East Cowes Castle. A persistent tradition holds that his coffin was carried across the surrounding fields at night in order to escape the attentions of his numerous creditors who, it was feared, planned to seize the coffin and its contents as a bizarre form of security. In fact his wife, Mary, was able to discharge all his debts within six years by selling off his properties before settling into a comfortable retirement in London.

his numerous creditors who, it was feared, planned to seize the coffin and its contents as a bizarre form of security

His obituaries were mixed in their appreciation of his work. The *Annual Register*[29] claimed, glumly and wrongly, that 'As a speculative builder this gentleman amassed a large fortune', but *John Bull* was more generous, referring to one of Nash's less well-known achievements, his redesign of St James's Park, while taking a sideswipe at less generous tributes to Nash:[30]

> 'Look at the manner in which the interior of St James's Park was, in a few months, converted from a swampy meadow into a luxurious garden and then let the reader ask himself, whether the metropolis is or is not indebted to the traduced object of this notice'.

A later age, which had had time to reflect upon his achievements in the capital, certainly appreciated Nash's work. During World War Two, many of Nash's Regent's Park terraces had, like other fine London buildings, been destroyed by bombing. After the war the Gorell

Commission[31] had to decide which monuments should be rebuilt as they were and which should be lost, given the serious shortage of building materials at that time. In 1946 they reported that:

'The Nash terraces are of national interest and importance ... they should be preserved as far as that is practicable and without strict regard to the economies of "prudent" estate management'.

View of Cornwall Terrace, Regent's Park, with figures, horses and carriages in the street, 1837. (By courtesy of the Guildhall Library, Corporation of London)

John Nash has few claims to originality as an architect. His designs were derivative and often hastily prepared, much of the detail being left to the architects or builders who executed his plans. However, his impact as a visionary planner on Regency London was unparalleled. At his death, in 1835, the Victorian age was approaching and London was ready to take up its place as the world's first metropolis and capital of the world's greatest empire.

Perhaps the last word on Nash should be left to an earlier writer. Henry Crabb Robinson (1775–1867) was a widely-travelled barrister who met Goethe and Schiller in Germany, became foreign editor of *The Times* and was a founder of University College London, so he was no *ingénue*. He recorded his impressions of a drive in Regent's Park in 1872:[32]

'I really think this enclosure, with the new street leading to it from Carlton House, will give a sort of glory to the Regent's government, which will be more felt by remote posterity than the victories of Trafalgar and Waterloo, glorious though these are'.

When Queen Victoria attempted to move into Buckingham Palace early in her reign she found that her uncle, George IV, and his favourite builder, John Nash, had left it an uninhabitable wreck. Thomas Cubitt, Victoria's favourite builder, had to rescue it from its derelict state. Yet Regent's Park, St James's Park and the thoroughfares that connected them remained as a permanent reminder that the reign of George IV was not without its redeeming features, expensive though they were.

[1] 17, Bloomsbury Square and 23–4, Great Russell Street.

[2] *Quarterly Review*, June 1826.

[3] *The Farington Diary*, edited by James Greig, Hutchinson, 1928, 7 November 1821, page 302.

[4] *First Report of His Majesty's Commissioners of Woods and Forests and Land Revenue*, 1812, Appendix XII.

[5] *First Report of His Majesty's Commissioners of Woods and Forests and Land Revenue*, 1812, page 10.

[6] Later known as the Grand Union Canal.

[7] *First Report of His Majesty's Commissioners of Woods and Forests and Land Revenue*, 1812, page 84.

[8] See Chapter 3 for an account of the work of Thomas Cubitt.

[9] French protestants; the origin of the term is mysterious.

[10] See Chapter 6 for an account of this strange episode.

[11] *First Report of His Majesty's Commissioners of Woods and Forests and Land Revenue*, 1812, page 89.

[12] *First Report of His Majesty's Commissioners of Woods and Forests and Land Revenue*, 1812, pages 88 and 89.

[13] Literally 'mallet to ball', an Italian term which reflects the game's origins.

[14] *George IV*, Michael De-la-Noy, Sutton Publishing, 1998, page 22.

[15] Parliamentary papers, 1828, volume 4, page 73.

[16] *Hansard*, 1 April 1824, column 35.

[17] *The Observer*, 31 March 1824.

[18] The Mystery Worshipper: http://ship-of-fools.com/Mystery/1998/006Mystery (website).

[19] *First Report of His Majesty's Commissioners of Woods and Forests and Land Revenue*, 1812, page 89.

[20] *The Farington Diary*, edited by James Greig, Hutchinson, 1928, 27 February 1821, page 275.

[21] See page 15 above.

[22] *Third Report of His Majesty's Commissioners of Woods and Forests and Land Revenue*, page 113.

[23] *The Builder*, 11 November 1848, page 548.

[24] *History of Regent Street*, Hermione Hobhouse, Macmillan, 1975, page 22.

[25] Parliamentary papers, 1828, volume 4, *Select Committee on Office of Works and Public Buildings*.

[26] See Chapter 3 for an account of Thomas Cubitt, Queen Victoria's builder.

[27] Parliamentary papers 1829, volume 3, page 39.

[28] *Hansard*, volume 21, column 1580 et seq. 25 May 1829.

[29] 1835 edition, page 221.

[30] 18 May 1835, page 156.

[31] *The Prime Minister's Commission on Regent's Park Terraces*, 1946, headed by Baron Gorell.

[32] *Diary, Reminiscences and Correspondence*, 1872, Henry Crabb Robinson, page 310.

CHAPTER 2

Marc and Isambard Kingdom Brunel and the Tunnelling Shield

'Of my own knowledge I can speak of the interest excited in foreign nations for the welfare and success of this undertaking; they look upon it as the greatest work of art ever contemplated'.
(The Duke of Wellington, July 1828, in a vain attempt to encourage his countrymen to invest in Marc Brunel's Thames Tunnel)

Marc Brunel. (By courtesy of the National Portrait Gallery, London)

The great big Duke of Wellington, in splendour on does reel,
And through the tunnel he will go, to buy some pickled eels.
(From a poem written to mark the opening of the Thames Tunnel, 1843)

ISAMBARD Kingdom Brunel (1806–59) is, perhaps, the most famous of all engineers with a legacy of railways, tunnels, ships and bridges. His father, Marc Isambard Brunel (1769–1849) is less well-known yet, like his famous son, he left a permanent mark on the history of England, and of London. He was the author of many valuable patents, made a significant contribution to the effectiveness of the Royal Navy during the Napoleonic Wars and was responsible for constructing the first world's first tunnel beneath a river, a tunnel which carries trains under the Thames to this day. The device he invented for the enterprise, the tunnelling shield, was later adapted to build the London underground railways.

A French Englishman

Marc was born in Normandy in 1769. His early education was at the hands of the distinguished mathematician, Gaspard Monge, who later became secretary to the French Navy under Napoleon. In 1792 he met his future wife, Sophia Kingdom. She was the granddaughter of a famous English clockmaker, Thomas Mudge, and had been sent to the Norman capital Rouen to learn French. It was the time of the Jacobin Terror and the two young people narrowly escaped execution when Marc unwisely prophesied the downfall of Robespierre in a Jacobin café in Paris.[1] Marc fled to the United States and Sophia to her native England. Marc became city engineer to the rapidly growing city of New York and later submitted a design for the new Capitol building in Washington, though another was chosen instead. In 1799 Marc returned to England and married Sophia. Their son, Isambard Kingdom Brunel, was born in April 1806.

submitted a design for the new Capitol building in Washington

The family into which the future engineer of the Great Western Railway was born was enterprising but penniless. During the course of his long life, Marc Brunel registered 17 patents, some of which, in the hands of a more provident man, would have brought him great wealth. In response to the exigencies of the Napoleonic Wars the Government ordered a major shipbuilding programme for the Royal Navy. One of the major bottlenecks in the construction of warships lay in the production of ships' blocks, the wooden blocks though which ropes were passed for raising, lowering and adjusting the direction of sails. Even a small vessel required several hundred of these devices, which had been made slowly and laboriously by hand. Marc patented a method of making them by machine, thereby removing this obstacle to the expansion of the Royal Navy and, in the process, enabling Nelson and his colleagues to destroy the French Navy, for which his old tutor, Gaspard Monge, was now responsible. Marc also invented an early typewriter, a cotton-winding machine, a knitting machine and a boot-making machine, the last of these being pressed into service to produce boots for the soldiers who were fighting Napoleon.

Marc's inventions earned him the prestigious rank of Fellow of the Royal Society, but unfortunately he was less than adept at exploiting them. He produced large stocks of army boots in response to orders from the War Office, which were cancelled when Napoleon abdicated, reinstated when he escaped from Elba and cancelled again after

Waterloo. The Admiralty, while grateful for the blocks which his machines had produced, showed a marked reluctance to pay for them. A further misfortune occurred when Marc's profitable sawmill in Battersea burned down, an event which led to the discovery that Marc's partner in the enterprise had been cheating him. In 1821, while his son Isambard was completing his formal education in France, Marc was committed to the King's Bench prison for debt. His faithful wife Sophia accompanied him there. A plea by Marc to the Admiralty to pay him the money due to him for his block-making machinery fell on deaf ears until he announced that he had written to Tsar Alexander of Russia offering to place himself, and his patents, at the service of that sovereign 'whose enlightenment and liberality seems to shine forth doubly in contrast with the callousness of the government at home'.[2] If this was a bluff, it worked. The government agreed to pay him £5,000 on condition that he stayed away from Russia. Marc agreed. His debts discharged, he emerged from prison and resumed his career as an inventor. In particular, he was able to turn his attention to a patent which he had registered three years before his temporary incarceration.

Marc was committed to the King's Bench prison for debt

Teredo navalis

During the time that he had spent in shipyards in connection with his work for the Admiralty Marc had become intrigued by the method by which the shipworm, or *teredo navalis*, tunnelled into the wooden ships. While it ate into the wood with its jaws its excrement hardened into a solid lining which prevented the resultant tunnel from collapsing and burying it.[3] This was a principle which, Marc realised, could be applied to the construction of tunnels through relatively unstable ground. It became the basis for the patent, number 4204, which he registered on 20 January 1818 for 'Forming drifts and tunnels underground'. The 'tunnelling shield' that resulted from the patent was devised in response to a long-felt need to construct a tunnel beneath the Thames below London Bridge, through the unstable sand, gravel and clay that was known to lie beneath the river. In 1802 the West India merchants had opened London's first enclosed docks, east of the Tower of London, on the Isle of Dogs, with berths for 600 ships. These were followed by the rapid growth of further docks on both sides of the Thames as London became the world's busiest port. This placed intolerable strain on London Bridge, the lowest point at which wheeled traffic could cross the river. It became the most congested place on earth. Almost a century would pass before Tower Bridge's famous bascules offered a lower crossing point above the river. In the meantime the prospect of a tunnel beneath the river was very attractive to the City merchants.

As the mining of coal and tin had developed in the late 18th century, techniques had been developed of excavating narrow tunnels through solid, stable rocks, the roofs supported by wooden pit props, but these methods were of no use when driving tunnels of larger diameter through soft subsoil. Several engineers had tried. An attempt to link Gravesend and Tilbury by tunnel in 1802 was abandoned in its early stages. In 1804 an enterprise known as the 'Thames Archway' came within less than a hundred feet of linking Rotherhithe and Limehouse before it was abandoned in the face of mounting costs and technical problems. In 1811 a further attempt was made, this time using brick cylinders which would be prefabricated on land, dropped into a trench in the river and sealed with a watertight joint. However, the watertight joint proved elusive and the project was abandoned.

Marc Brunel's solution to the problem consisted of a rectangular frame or shield, roughly 21 feet high and 36 feet wide. The shield was divided into 36 compartments on three levels, each level holding 12 compartments. The shield would be set against the ground that was to be excavated. Each of the 36 compartments, roughly seven feet high, three feet wide and six feet deep, would contain a 'miner' who would excavate the ground before him with pick and shovel, passing the earth that he had hacked out to other miners behind him who would remove it from the tunnel for disposal elsewhere. All the miners were protected from falling earth by the frame itself. When a sufficient volume of earth had been dug out by each miner the shield itself would be pushed forward by screw jacks and the miner would begin work on the next section. In the meantime bricklayers would follow behind, lining the tunnel as the shield advanced. Marc described his invention in *A New Plan of Tunnelling, calculated for opening a Roadway under the Thames*,[4] and explained it to a gathering at the Institution of Civil Engineers on 17 February 1824, where it was received with enthusiasm. Marc's plan required the sinking of two shafts, the first at Rotherhithe on the south bank of the Thames, the second at Wapping on the north bank. These would be linked by a tunnel 1,200 feet long which would descend gradually as it left each bank, reaching its lowest point in the middle of the river where the Thames was deepest. It was hoped that the tunnel workings would be protected from flooding by the belt of clay which, Marc believed, ran at an appropriate depth beneath the channel of the river. The tunnel would contained two arched carriageways, one for each direction, and these would be separated by a dividing wall in which open arches would give access to the neighbouring carriageway.

The day after his presentation to the civil engineers Marc held a public meeting at the City of London Tavern, Bishopsgate, at which

Each of the 36 compartments, roughly seven feet high, three feet wide and six feet deep, would contain a 'miner'

members of the audience were invited to subscribe to the Thames Tunnel Company. The City of London Tavern was a traditional venue for raising money for such enterprises. A few years later it would be used for the same purpose by the promoters of the London Metropolitan Railway. On this occasion Marc succeeded in raising £179,000 for his new enterprise.[5] The subscribers included many well-informed and well-connected men of the time: Edward Baring of Baring's bank; Benjamin Hawes, later Secretary of War; and the engineering Bramahs, descendants of Joseph Bramah, whose many inventions included the Victorian water-closet and an unpickable lock. The chairman of the Thames Tunnel Company was to be a well-connected MP called William Smith. Smith was to create problems for Marc when the tunnel ran into difficulties and the two men lost faith in each other. For the moment, however, there was clearly a great deal of confidence in Marc Brunel's project.

The shield, weighing 80 tons in all, was constructed in 12 cast-iron sections at the South London works of the pioneering engineer Henry Maudslay, in whose works Marc's son Isambard had already gained some experience. There was no engineer better qualified than Maudslay to make such a novel device. However, the shield first had to be put in place and for this Marc developed a novel method of constructing the first shaft. An iron cylinder, 50 feet in diameter and three feet high, was placed on the ground at Rotherhithe. The lower side of the cylinder, in contact with the ground, had been sharpened so that it would cut into the earth. The brick walls of the shaft were

An iron cylinder, 50 feet in diameter and three feet high, was placed on the ground at Rotherhithe

HENRY MAUDSLAY (1771–1831)

Henry Maudslay was a pioneer in the manufacture and use of machine tools. He was born at Woolwich in 1771 where he worked as a 14-year-old boy in the carpenter's and blacksmith's shops. In 1780 he was engaged by the famous inventor Joseph Bramah[6] as a toolmaker. In 1797, after an argument with Bramah about wages, he set up his own workshop in Oxford Street, London, where he proceeded to turn out a stream of innovative machine tools: lathes; flour and saw mills; machinery for minting coins; screw-cutting lathes and a device for punching holes in iron and steel, among many others. He was the obvious choice for Marc Brunel when Marc sought someone to manufacture his tunnelling shield, though the contract to make the later, stronger shield was won from Maudslay by the Rennie brothers. One of his descendants founded the Standard motor company.

then built on the upper side of the cylinder which, in effect, formed the shaft's foundations. When the brick walls of the shaft had reached their required height above the ground workmen then began to dig out the earth within and beneath the ring, shovelling the excavated earth into a continuous chain of buckets which were raised to the surface by steam. As the men excavated, the shaft sank beneath the weight of the bricks and its downward progress became one of London's great visitor attractions, the Duke of Wellington himself being among the first to view the spectacle. By June 1825 it had reached the required depth some 80 feet below high-water mark. Marc wanted to excavate a sump beneath the shaft that could be used to drain water from the tunnel workings as they advanced to the opposite shore. This would have been both a valuable safety device

its downward progress became one of London's great visitor attractions

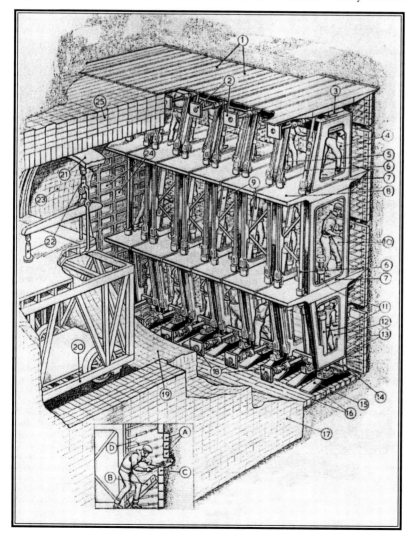

Marc Brunel's tunnelling shield.

and a good investment, since the tunnel was to suffer from frequent flooding, but the chairman, William Smith, opposed it on grounds of economy. In November 1825 the tunnelling shield was in place and tunnelling could finally begin.

Isambard Kingdom Brunel, resident engineer

Marc employed a resident engineer to oversee work on the site but the first, George Armstrong, suffered a breakdown in his health in August 1826, shortly after the shield came into operation, probably from overwork. Marc's 20-year old son Isambard now took over the task. There were many difficulties encountered in teaching the miners to use the new shield and to work as a team so that the advancement of the shield was not held up owing to differences in the pace of work among the 36 men engaged at any one time. Isambard Kingdom's training and, above all, his determination, made him well suited to the formidable task which he had now taken on.

In September 1817 as an 11-year-old boy, Isambard had been sent by Marc to stay with his older cousin in France, where, Marc believed, he would receive a better education in applied mathematics than was available in England. He was sent to a college in Caen, Normandy, and later to the famous Lycée Henri IV in Paris, which then, as now, prepared clever boys for entrance to the Ecole Polytechnique, where engineers were trained for the public service. However, Isambard, as an English citizen, could not proceed to the Ecole Polytechnique. He went instead to work for a famous French clockmaker, Louis Breguet, where he learned about precision engineering. It was during this period that Marc was in the King's Bench prison. In 1822 Isambard returned to England and spent some time gaining experience

Isambard Kingdom Brunel, who became resident engineer on the Thames Tunnel in 1826, aged 20, before becoming the most famous engineer of his age. (By courtesy of the National Portrait Gallery, London)

with Henry Maudslay, whose company was later chosen to manufacture Marc Brunel's shield.

Isambard's appointment as resident engineer in August 1826 was followed by more rapid progress in the tunnelling, although this was accompanied by problems. The shield was buckled and there occurred the first in a series of incidents which were to bedevil the tunnel's progress: the seepage of water into the tunnel from the river above. The layer of clay that was supposed to protect the workings was not thick enough. In May 1827 a greater volume of water began to leak into the tunnel, together with bits of glass and other detritus that could only have come from the river. By this date the Thames been receiving an increasing proportion of London's sewage[7] for 12 years, so its waters posed a risk to the health of those working in the tunnel even if it did not threaten to drown them. Tunnelling ceased and Isambard hired a diving bell with which to inspect the workings. This was, literally, an open-mouthed bell equipped with seats around its top. Candle-lit, it was lowered into the water. The entry of water from the river was limited only by the pressure of air as the water level rose. Isambard was lowered into the Thames above the area where he believed the tunnel was being breached. He was accompanied by his redoubtable mother, though his father, whose health was being affected by the tunnel's troubles, remained ashore. By this hazardous process, performed on more than one occasion, he located the breach and arranged for it to be sealed with bags of clay. The water was then pumped out and Isambard entered the tunnel on a punt, which was propelled to the point where the river had deposited its foul load on and around the precious shield. He then left the punt, crawled over the bank of slime and, by candlelight, established that the shield, though misaligned, could be brought back into use. He then returned via the same route. Isambard Kingdom Brunel was a 'hands-on' engineer!

In October tunnelling resumed after a six-month delay which was causing great alarm to the chairman, William Smith, who was losing confidence in Marc Brunel's judgement. Shareholders' funds were running out and this was a time of great anxiety for father and son. Further worry for Marc was caused by the decision of the directors to raise some cash by admitting spectators to the tunnel to watch the work in progress, charging them a shilling each. Marc feared that accidents would result. In August he had suffered a breakdown in his health and Isambard made notes in his journal which reflected both an awareness of his weaknesses and the determination that he now displayed in his efforts to complete the task. On 19 October 1827, he wrote 'My self-conceit renders me domineering, intolerant, nay even

'My self-conceit renders me domineering, intolerant, nay even quarrelsome'

quarrelsome' but he added 'Be the first Engineer and example for all future ones'. He later reflected on the embarrassments and failures of the tunnel compared with the glories being achieved by his contemporaries the Rennie brothers, also sons of a famous father, who were at that time engaged on the construction of London Bridge:

> 'The young Rennies – whatever their real merit – will have built London Bridge, the finest bridge in Europe … while I have been engaged on the tunnel which failed, a pretty recommendation'.[8]

Further setbacks were at hand. In January 1828 there was a disastrous flood. Isambard himself was on the shield supervising the work when the water flooded in and he narrowly avoided being drowned. He was hauled, unconscious, from the workings. Six workers were not so lucky. They lost their lives. The tunnel was barely half-completed and shareholders' funds were exhausted. Despairing attempts were made to attract new investors. The Duke of Wellington, then Prime Minister, gave his support, assuring his countrymen:

> 'Of my own knowledge I can speak of the interest excited in foreign nations for the welfare and success of this undertaking; they look upon it as the greatest work of art ever contemplated'.

The Iron Duke backed his words with his own money but very few of his countrymen followed his example. Only £9,600 was subscribed by investors of the £200,000 required.[9] In August the tunnel was closed. The only hope now lay in an advance from the Government. Six years passed before the personal antagonisms which had begun to afflict the project were resolved and in the meantime *The Times*, tired of the delays, accidents and problems which had kept the tunnel in the headlines, began to refer to it as 'The Great Bore'. Thomas Hood, in his *Ode to Monsieur Brunel* advised Marc to use the tunnel as a wine cellar. The tunnel had reached its lowest fortunes.

The Times *began to refer to it as 'The Great Bore'.*

Marc Brunel vindicated

A series of fresh proposals were now considered for completing the tunnel while approaches were made to the Government for support from the Exchequer Loan Commission – an organisation backed by the Treasury which was permitted to make loans for the completion of works which were in the public interest. Such loans were very rare at a time when *laissez-faire* economic doctrines were taking hold and when there was no tradition of public investment in public amenities. It was therefore essential that plans for completing the tunnel enjoyed the confidence of the Government so, to that end, the Tunnel Company referred the different proposals for finishing the tunnel to a committee of distinguished engineers. They included James Walker, president of the Institution of Civil Engineers; Peter Barlow, who later developed the tunnelling shield for the construction of underground railways; William Tierney Clark, a pioneering water engineer; and the professor of mathematics from the new University College, London, Augustus de Morgan. This formidable quartet duly endorsed Brunel's method as the most feasible one for completing the tunnel and, fortified by this vote of confidence in their engineer, the directors approached the Government for a loan. They were surprised to discover that an earlier tentative offer by the Government had been quietly rejected by their chairman, William Smith, who was motivated by a desire to get rid of Marc Brunel and find another engineer more to his liking. Smith was sacked as chairman and, after further delays, a government loan was made to the company in December, 1834.

Marc now designed a new, more robust shield to replace the damaged one and in March 1836, six and a half years after work had ceased, tunnelling began again. Over the next two and a half years there were three serious floods and many minor ones. A further problem was the leakage into the tunnel of noxious gases such as hydrogen sulphide and firedamp. The tunnellers were now burrowing through unstable ground, saturated with sewage from the polluted Thames, and inhaling poisonous gases. At times their nostrils were surrounded with filthy, black accretions. There was a steady stream of engineers, foremen and miners to Guy's Hospital and Marc's diary recorded regular fainting fits and vomiting among his workforce, punctuated by frequent explosions of firedamp. Every two hours, day and night, Marc visited the tunnel office to check the latest reports on the state of the ground. So worried was his wife Sophia by the effect on the health of her 70-year-old husband that she rigged up a rope with a bell and bucket outside his bedroom window. Every two hours the bell rang, Marc awoke and pulled up the bucket with the latest samples of earth for his inspection.

He placed his instructions in the bucket which was lowered to the ground as he returned to his rest. It must have come as some consolation to Marc that he had at least earned the approval of Queen Victoria, who in March 1841 conferred a knighthood on her long-suffering engineer.

These ordeals were accompanied by further requests to the Government for financial aid. At this time James Walker's attitude to

At times their nostrils were surrounded with filthy, black accretions

the project was critical to its success. As President of the Institution of Civil Engineers he was the recognised head of the profession and without his support the scheme would have foundered. He told the Treasury of his confidence in Brunel's competence:

'*as the Thames Tunnel is Mr Brunel's work as respects design and responsibility any measure that may be proposed for executing the work should, in my judgement, have his approval*'.[10]

Government loans eventually amounted to £250,000. In December, 1841, after three more floods, the tunnel finally reached the northern shore at Wapping where a shaft had already been sunk to receive it. In the meantime, in November 1842, as the finishing touches were being made to the tunnel, Marc suffered a stroke.

Fortunately Marc was sufficiently recovered to attend the tunnel opening ceremony on 25 March 1843. This was a very grand occasion. A military band played *See The Conquering Hero Comes* as a long procession was led through the tunnel by a metropolitan policeman proudly wearing a medal that signified that he had fought at Waterloo. The cheering crowds were evidently not distracted by the only sour note of the day. This was sounded by Thames watermen who flew black flags to signify the destitution which they feared would be caused by their loss of trade to the tunnel. The occasion also inspired some poetry of very doubtful quality including the following verse composed by one John Morgan.

The great big Duke of Wellington, in splendour on does reel,
And through the tunnel he will go, to buy some pickled eels,
Both horse and man can go by land, oh, what a pretty game,
From Rotherhithe to Wapping, underneath the river Thames.

This is the only record of the Iron Duke's devotion to pickled eels

This is the only record of the Iron Duke's devotion to pickled eels. The reader is unlikely to find the poem in any anthology of English verse.[11]

Tunnel or fairground?

In its first four months more than a million pedestrians visited the tunnel, most of them drawn by curiosity rather than by a need to cross the river. In the first full year the number reached two million. Each of them paid a penny to do so but the income yielded by these visitors, amounting to less than £9,000, came nowhere near paying the interest on the loan from the Government, let alone the capital invested by the shareholders. It had originally been anticipated that the tunnel would

The Thames Tunnel.
(London's Transport
Museum)

accommodate carriages, for which sixpence would have been charged, but as all the available capital was exhausted in constructing the pedestrian stairways this potentially profitable source of revenue was lost.

The directors therefore resorted to other methods in an attempt to make the tunnel pay. Even before the tunnel opened the directors had admitted visitors to those parts which were completed in return for a payment of as much as a shilling and soon after its official opening they permitted stallholders to occupy the arches which linked the northbound and southbound passageways. In July 1843 Queen Victoria visited the tunnel. The *Illustrated London News*, having recorded that 'the company was more numerous than select' among the East End coal porters and bargees, reported that one gallant

one gallant stallholder, selling silken goods, emulated Sir Walter Raleigh

stallholder, selling silken goods, emulated Sir Walter Raleigh when he 'displayed his loyalty in a peculiar manner. All the silk handkerchiefs disposed on his stall for sale were removed and placed on the ground for Her Majesty to pass over'.[12] In April 1844, a year after the opening, the company mounted the first of many 'Fancy Fairs', and these became a feature of the tunnel in its first 20 years – it thereby developed into a visitor attraction rather than a means of communication. Stallholders came from afar to sell food, drink, trinkets and souvenirs. Some of the stalls became a permanent fixture, paying an annual rent of a few pounds to the Tunnel Company. One entrepreneur came from Leipzig and affixed a notice to his stall announcing 'hier spricht man Deutsch' ('German spoken here'). Guidebooks to the tunnel were printed in all the major European languages and one writer, in 1853, recorded his impressions of a visit:[13]

'As we descend, stray bits of music greet our ears … the passages which communicate between the two roadways are tenanted by a numerous race of small shopkeepers, offering views of the tunnel and other penny wares for sale. As we proceed the music becomes more clear and distinct … It is an Italian organ played by a perfect doll of a Lilliputian machine…The Marsellaise, German Waltzes, the Hungarian Rakowzy March, Rule Britannia, Yankee Doodle Dandy etc … You also see a Spanish convent and the Emperor Napoleon in the act of being beaten at Waterloo'.

An engineering triumph; a financial disaster

In its heyday the tunnel was London's principal gift shop,[14] frequented by tourists as well as Londoners rather as Oxford Street and Knightsbridge are visited now. Souvenirs featuring the tunnel itself were numerous and popular. *Spooner's Protean Views* included a holograph-like picture which changed from the Thames Tunnel to the Coronation Procession as it was held at different angles to the light. Even the tunnel's misfortunes were exploited in this way, with a 'peep show' illustrating the disastrous floods of May 1827, and the sealing of the breach with bags of clay. But this period of modest prosperity was short-lived and the stallholders' rents never contributed more than a few hundred pounds a year to the empty coffers of the Tunnel Company and its long-suffering shareholders. By 1860 the tunnel had degenerated into a haunt of homeless tramps, drunks and prostitutes, which respectable Londoners hesitated to visit.

In the meantime the company's debts continued to mount. Since the revenue was inadequate to pay even the interest on the Treasury loan the size of the loan grew rather than diminished. By 1865 this debt had grown from £250,000 to £393,666. In the meantime the shareholders had received no dividends at all. In that year the tunnel was bought by the East London Railway.

a haunt of homeless tramps, drunks and prostitutes

A railway tunnel

The purpose of this early addition to the London Underground was to link the main line railways north and south of the river, though this aim was never successfully accomplished owing to the poor connections to the main lines to the north. It opened in 1869 between New Cross and Wapping via the Thames Tunnel but it never ran its own trains. Its services were operated from the south by main line companies which were later incorporated into the Southern Railway. From the north its services were run by the Metropolitan and the District Railways. The East London Railway was even less successful as a commercial venture than the Thames Tunnel through which it ran. It ran into difficulties through placing its finances in the hands of a colourful figure called Albert Grant, who had a gift for applying shareholders' money to his own needs and later used some of his ill-gotten gains to refurbish Leicester Square. In May 1878 Sir Edward Watkin was appointed as receiver to the line, later becoming its chairman. He brought about some modest revival in its fortunes and attempted to include it in his grand scheme for a railway from Manchester to Paris, crossing the Thames by the Thames Tunnel and reaching France via a Channel Tunnel which he started to build, ceasing only when Parliament ordered him to do so. In 1925 the Thames Tunnel passed to the Southern Railway and in 1948 it passed to the London Underground, with whom it remains. Its continued use

The East London Railway. (*Illustrated London News*)

of Brunel's tunnel enables this otherwise obscure railway to claim the distinction of running through the world's oldest tunnel cut beneath a river. The tale of Sir Edward Watkin's ambitions is told in more detail in Chapter 7.

Tunnelling shields

Marc Brunel's invention of the tunnelling shield transformed both the methods and the possibilities of creating wide-gauge tunnels. Marc himself died in 1849, six years after his tunnel opened, but later engineers built upon his experience and example to create new shield designs which, though more sophisticated, were clearly based on his model. The first was Peter Barlow (1809–85), one of the quartet who, in 1830, had given the vote of confidence to Brunel's methods which had helped to secure the Treasury loan.[15] Barlow replaced Marc Brunel's rectangular shield with a cylindrical design that could be used to excavate a circular tunnel for an underground railway. Marc Brunel's original patent of 1818[16] had been for a cylindrical shield with rotating, steam-powered blades to excavate the earth. He had realised that no steam engine of the time would be powerful enough to drive the blades so he substituted a rectangular shield designed to hold human excavators. Ironically his original cylindrical design was literally the shape of things to come.

Peter Barlow used this method to build the 'Tower Subway', which runs 400 yards beneath the Thames from Tower Hill to Pickleherring Street, a road which vanished in the 20th century but was opposite the present mooring of HMS *Belfast*.[17] The subway opened on 7 August 1870. First-class passengers paid twopence and second-class passengers a penny to be drawn across the river while sitting in carriages which ran on a 2ft 6in gauge track. A cable was attached to the carriages and this was pulled by a stationary steam engine on the

THE BARLOW BROTHERS

Each of the Barlow brothers made an important contribution to railway history. In 1862 Peter Barlow (1809–85) was sinking cast-iron cylinders into the Thames to build the old Lambeth suspension bridge when he conceived the idea of turning the cylinders on their sides to form a tunnel *beneath* the river. From this he developed the idea of a cylindrical tunnelling shield which could be used to excavate a circular tunnel slightly larger than the prefabricated iron segments (in place of Marc Brunel's brickwork) which would be bolted into place as the shield advanced. This was the first cylindrical tunnelling shield to enter use. His younger brother William Henry Barlow (1812–1902) worked as an engineer on the Manchester and Birmingham Railway and later designed and built the Midland Railway line to London. He also designed the railway's St Pancras terminal, including the huge iron and glass span of its famous train shed, which remained the widest span of its kind for a quarter of a century.

shore. In its first few months the curiosity value of the subway, London's first real 'tube', attracted a number of inquisitive passengers, just as the Thames Tunnel had done. However, the proximity of the toll-free London Bridge ensured that the venture was no more successful than its predecessor had been. In 1870 a receiver was appointed, the railway was removed and the subway became a foot tunnel carrying a million pedestrians a year. Peter Barlow thereafter devoted himself to writing articles and pamphlets whose titles reveal their purpose: removing further threats to his subway. One such pamphlet was called *The Tower Bridge: observations to prove that a new bridge east of London Bridge is unnecessary*.[18] Fortunately Barlow's attempts to vilify Sir Joseph Bazalgette's proposal for a new Tower Bridge failed, and after the latter opened in 1894 the subway was closed to pedestrians.[19] It remains in use, conducting water and power lines beneath the Thames.

The first real 'tube'

Fortunately Peter Barlow had other, more promising, ideas in prospect. He began to campaign for a 'City and Southwark Subway', over a mile in length, to link the City of London with the Elephant and Castle. The line soon changed both its name and its length. It was extended to Stockwell and became the City and South London Railway. In 1924 it became part of the Northern Line. Barlow's assistant in the project was James Henry Greathead (1844–96), who was to push the tunnelling shield one step further. Greathead was a South African who had come to England when he was 15 and worked as an assistant to Barlow in the construction of the Tower Subway. He had developed a shield which, while incorporating Barlow's cylindrical design, also incorporated sharp steel blades which were forced into the clay by hydraulic rams at a pressure of a ton per square inch. Miners then removed the loosened clay. This speeded up the tunnelling and was the basis of future shield technology. The shield could also be steered to left or right, up or down, by applying varying pressures to the rams around the circumference of the shield.

Tunnelling began in May 1886, from a shaft sunk into the river west of London Bridge.[20] From that point one tunnel headed north to a terminus in King William Street[21] and the other south towards Stockwell. The shield enabled tunnelling to be done 40 feet or more below the surface, well below sewers and foundations, to forestall any damage claims from property owners. The tunnels were 10ft 2in diameter, which was to cause problems later when the railway was incorporated in what became the Northern Line. Other 'tubes', built later, were to a gauge of 11ft 8in, so the City and South London had to be re-engineered in 1923–4 in order to enable rolling stock of wider gauge to be used throughout the system.

Besides the newly designed shield the City and South London Railway incorporated another innovation: electric traction. London's earliest underground railways, the Metropolitan and the District, had been built just below street level. They were drawn by steam locomotives and ventilated, in theory, by shafts in the streets above. The system was far from satisfactory, leaving *passengers choking in fuming tunnels*, and it clearly wouldn't work in tunnels 40 feet below the surface. The directors of the company had originally planned to use cable cars, using a method developed by a Londoner called Andrew Hallidie and applied by him in 1871 to San Francisco's cable cars. The system was marketed in England by the Patent Cable Tramways Corporation. Trains would attach themselves to a continuously moving cable, detaching themselves when they wanted to stop at a station. Greathead advocated this system, which would presumably have resulted in a very jerky ride, but he began to have doubts about the wisdom of the system as the railway lengthened to three and a half miles along a route with many bends. His doubts were resolved when, in 1888, the Patent Cable Tramways Corporation became bankrupt.

passengers choking in fuming tunnels

The City and South London's small electric locomotives struggled, lights flickering, up the incline to King William Street station.
(London's Transport Museum)

The company's directors then took the bold step of deciding to adopt electric traction instead. A power station was built at Stockwell and 14 locomotives were purchased, each capable of running at 25 miles per hour on 450 volts of current. A train consisted of three wooden carriages known as 'padded cells' on account of their lavish upholstery and tiny, slit-like windows, situated just below the carriage roof.[22] The latter were adopted because the directors feared that passengers would become alarmed if they had too clear a view of the tunnel walls rushing past. The railway was opened on 4 November 1890 by the Prince of Wales and passengers immediately noticed other novel features. It was the first railway to use lifts to take passengers to and from station platforms and the first to have only one class of travel. The latter became the normal pattern for underground railways, though at the time one writer disapproved, commenting that 'we have scarcely yet been educated up to that condition of social equality when lords and ladies will be content to ride side by side with Billingsgate "fish fags" and Smithfield butchers'.[23]

The City and South London Railway was a triumphant feat of engineering both in its use of shield technology and in its adoption of electric traction. It was extremely popular with passengers, over five million using it during its first full year of operation at a flat fare of twopence. On occasion its little locomotives struggled to pull their

The City and South London's 'padded cells', whose small, roof-level windows were so designed to prevent passengers becoming alarmed as the tunnel walls flashed past. (London's Transport Museum)

lords and ladies will be content to ride side by side with Billingsgate "fish fags" and Smithfield butchers

Opening of Stockwell station on the City and South London Railway, 1890. Note the dome for the lift mechanism – a novel device. (London's Transport Museum)

over-laden coaches up the incline towards King William Street station. Lights flickered as the electric current struggled to cope with the demands placed upon it and trains sometimes had to reverse to beyond the bottom of the incline and take another run at it. But despite its popularity with passengers it failed to offer a reasonable return to its investors. It paid no dividend for the first year and after seven years was paying only two per cent – no more than the bank rate.

The Price Rotary Excavator

Within 15 years a further development in tunnelling technology was achieved by a British engineer called John Price. He designed a shield that incorporated electrically powered rotating knives, which delivered the excavated earth straight on to a conveyor belt. Picks and shovels now assumed a minor role as the new technology drove the Charing Cross, Euston and Hampstead Railway north to Golders Green at unprecedented speeds and greater depths than ever before. This eventually became the northern arm of the Northern Line. The London underground railway reached its greatest depth just north of

John Price's rotary excavator – lineal descendent of Marc Brunel's original design. (London's Transport Museum)

Hampstead station, 221 feet below Hampstead Heath. Greathead shields were still used for tunnelling through awkward, waterlogged ground.

Despite the technical advances, tunnelling remained a dangerous business. The builders of the Bakerloo line, in the first years of the 20th century, encountered the same problems that Marc Brunel had faced when they, like him, tried to tunnel beneath the Thames: leakage of water from waterlogged soil. Their solution was to seal the tunnels and the shafts leading to them with airlocks and pump compressed air into the airtight chamber until the pressure was sufficient to hold the water at bay in the surrounding soil. The technique had harmful effects upon the tunnellers, who suffered from 'the bends' when they returned to normal atmospheric pressure. These were casually mentioned in a paper to the Institution of Civil Engineers in 1908 which described the Bakerloo tunnelling:

there were not many fatal cases

'*The tunnel was being driven under a pressure of 35 pounds per square inch for a considerable distance [normal atmospheric pressure at sea level is 15 pounds psi]; a great deal of illness resulted among the men but **there were not many fatal cases** [author's bold!]. The air escaping through the gravelly bed of the river boiled three feet high above the surface. It came in the path of a race from Charing Cross to Putney and upset one of the competitors' boats*'.[24]

The speaker reassured his audience that compensation had been paid to the aggrieved boat owners, but clearly accepted the illness and mortality among the unfortunate tunnellers as a normal hazard.

In the 1960s, when the Victoria Line was being built, further refinements of Price's design enabled 470 feet of tunnel to be bored in one week, yet when waterlogged soil was encountered between Pimlico and Brixton the engineers reverted to a mixture of traditional methods while using new materials. The waterlogged ground was frozen with tubes of liquid nitrogen, enabling the tunnellers to work their way through firm terrain and a Greathead shield was employed, using manual labour: a method which Marc Brunel would easily have recognised. Further refinements in shield design were incorporated in the equipment that was used to build the Jubilee Line and, of course, the Channel Tunnel, but if Marc Brunel had been present he would have recognised both the equipment and the methods as descended from his original conception.

Postscript: Paddington Station

Isambard Kingdom Brunel outlived his father by only 10 years, dying in September 1859. However, this gave him time to make his own lasting contribution to the fabric of London: Paddington Station. He had been engineer to the Great Western Railway since 1833 and by 1838 a temporary terminus at Bishop's Road, west of the present site of Paddington station, was opened to run trains as far as Maidenhead. This wooden structure was never intended as a permanent terminus though it was the one to which Queen Victoria and Prince Albert made their inaugural journey from Windsor in June 1842. The engineer Daniel Gooch drove the locomotive *Phlegothon* on that auspicious occasion, achieving an average speed of 44mph with the locomotive that he had himself designed. Any pride that he felt at reaching a speed which far exceeded any that the Queen had previously experienced would have been wounded by Albert's request that, in future, Her Majesty would prefer to travel much more slowly. The Queen had been thoroughly frightened by the experience and for the rest of her reign royal trains proceeded at a much more stately pace. A station at Bishop's Road remained in use. In 1863 it formed the western

in future, Her Majesty would prefer to travel much more slowly

---

DANIEL GOOCH (1816–1889)

Daniel Gooch was born in Northumberland and from an early age worked in the locomotive works of George Stephenson and his son Robert. In 1837 he was appointed locomotive superintendent to the Great Western Railway, where he worked with the formidable I.K. Brunel and designed the fastest and most powerful locomotives that had ever been produced up to that time. Over 500 locomotives were built to his designs. He designed a special 'condensing engine' for the early underground railways which emitted less steam and smoke in the enclosed tunnels of the Metropolitan Railway. In 1864 he resigned from the Great Western to pursue interests in telegraphic communications. He bought Brunel's ship the *Great Eastern* at a bankruptcy sale and tried to lay the first submarine cable between Ireland and Newfoundland. In August 1865, after 1,200 miles had been laid, Gooch witnessed the cable breaking and sinking without trace. In the same year he became MP for Cricklade and remained in Parliament for 20 years, never making a speech in the House of Commons. On his death in 1889 his estate was valued at £750,000 – 10 times that of his mentor Brunel.

terminus of the Metropolitan Railway, the world's first underground railway, running to Farringdon in the heart of the City.[25] It remained Paddington (Bishop's Road) until 1933 when it was incorporated in one Paddington underground station.

In the meantime the search continued for a permanent site for the terminus. The possible choice of a site in Pimlico caused some anxiety to Thomas Cubitt as he set about turning the area from a swamp into a pleasant residential area[26] and a shared terminus with the London and Birmingham Railway at Euston was considered for a while before being rejected. It was not until 1853 that the Great Western directors sanctioned the construction of a permanent terminus on the present site. Brunel had been determined upon such a course for years and in 1851, in a characteristic letter, he wrote to the architect Matthew Digby Wyatt inviting him to join Brunel in the enterprise while leaving no doubt about who would be the senior partner:[27]

> 'I am going to design, in a great hurry, a station after my own fancy [and] of course believe myself fully competent; but for detail of ornamentation I
> neither have time nor knowledge ... Are you willing to enter upon the work professionally in the subordinate capacity ... I shall expect you at 9 ½ this evening'.

Brunel was a notorious workaholic, routinely working 18 hours a day and sleeping in the 'Britzka carriage' which was designed to convey him from one task to the next while he worked or, occasionally, slept. Wyatt led a more measured existence but presumably he attended punctually, as required, and accepted the 'subordinate capacity' to which he had been allocated by Brunel, since the Moorish motifs which decorated the iron columns supporting the station roof were his. However the iron and glass structure of the station was undoubtedly Brunel's. Brunel was one of the committee that was responsible for choosing a design for the building for the Great Exhibition of 1851, the year in which this letter was written. He had even played a part in designing the committee's own proposal for the building – a design which had provoked wide criticism. It says much for Brunel that he was one of the first to recognise the superiority of Sir Joseph Paxton's Crystal Palace[28] and he later played an active part in the relocation of the building to south London. Brunel's design for Paddington Station reflects his admiration of Paxton's work. Paddington was the first main line station to make such imaginative use of a large metal frame with glass panels. The whole area was covered with three spans of 70 feet, 102 feet and 68 feet. This design for a major station was to be followed by many railway engineers in the years that followed, most notably at St Pancras, where the 240-foot span came into use in 1868, 14 years after Brunel's Paddington. The designer of St Pancras was William Barlow, brother of the Peter Barlow who had supported Marc Brunel's application for government help to complete the Thames Tunnel, and who had later played an important role in creating the City and South London Railway.[29] Brunel's station was the first to have a major hotel attached to it: the Great Western Hotel designed by Philip Hardwick who later went on to design Euston Station.

Thus did Marc and Isambard Kingdom Brunel leave their marks on Victorian London, the first below ground and the second above. Both of the great works with which their names are associated, the Thames Tunnel and Paddington Station, involved pioneering use of machinery and materials and both remain in daily use bearing passengers to and from the city and carrying them beneath its river. Both the tunnel and the station were regarded by contemporaries with wonder. In the 1830s thousands of people paid a shilling to visit the world's first tunnel beneath a river. Thirty years later 21,150 visitors each paid a shilling to see a 10-foot painting by W.P. Frith called 'The Railway Station'. The painting, of Paddington, showed the feverish activity of a railway station[30]. Like the Thames Tunnel the great Victorian railway station was a wonder of the world.

[1] *Brunel's Tunnel*, A. Mathewson and D. Laval, Brunel Exhibition Rotherhithe, 1992, page 9, describes this incident.

[2] *Isambard Kingdom Brunel, Engineering Knight-Errant*, Adrian Vaughan, John Murray, 1991, page 8 recounts this episode.

[3] *The Tunnel*, by David Lampe, Harrap, 1963, page 30.

[4] Printed By Richard Taylor of Shoe Lane, *c.*1823; this episode is described in *The Triumphant Bore*, the Institution of Civil Engineers, 1993; the most thorough account of the construction of the tunnel.

[5] For a roughly equivalent sum for the 21st century multiply this sum by 1,000: i.e. £179m.

[6] See page 128 below for an account of the work of Joseph Bramah.

[7] See Chapter 6 pages 128 et seq. for an account of this development.

[8] *Isambard Kingdom Brunel, Engineering Knight-Errant*, Adrian Vaughan, John Murray, 1991, pages 28-31 give these quotations from I.K. Brunel's *Journal*.

[9] *Brunel's Tunnel*, A. Mathewson and D. Laval, Brunel Exhibition Rotherhithe, 1992, page 32.

[10] *The Triumphant Bore*, the Institution of Civil Engineers, 1993, page 43.

[11] *The Triumphant Bore*, the Institution of Civil Engineers, 1993, page 31, contains the poem in full.

[12] *Illustrated London News*, 29 July 1843, page 75.

[13] *Sauntering in and about London*, by Max Schlesinger, London, 1853, page 144.

[14] *The Triumphant Bore*, the Institution of Civil Engineers, 1993, page 22.

15 See page 41 above for this reference.
16 See page 34 above.
17 See *Railway Magazine* (89), 1943, p332 et seq. for an article on the Tower Subway by Charles E. Lee.
18 Spon, 1878, available in the Metropolitan Archives ref. P.27.52.
19 See Chapters 5 and 6 for an account of the planning and building of Tower Bridge.
20 The engineering work is described in *The Engineer*, 7 June 1889, pages 477–8.
21 This station, now no longer served by trains, is used for document storage.
22 One of these 'padded cells' may be seen in London's Transport Museum, Covent Garden.
23 *Railway Times*, 8 November 1890, page 545.
24 *Minutes of Proceedings*, Institution of Civil Engineers, vol. 175, 1908–9, page 214.
25 See Chapter 7 for an account of the Metropolitan Railway.
26 See Chapter 3 for an account of Cubitt's work in Pimlico.
27 *Isambard Kingdom Brunel*, L.T.C. Rolt, Penguin, 1989, page 301.
28 See Chapter 4 for an account of Paxton's Crystal Palace.
29 See page 46 for an account of the Barlow brothers.
30 The painting is now at Royal Holloway College, Egham.

CHAPTER 3

Thomas Cubitt: Queen Victoria's Builder

'A better, kinderhearted or more simple, unassuming man never breathed'.

(Queen Victoria, writing of Thomas Cubitt, builder of Osborne House and much of 19th century London)

'The great struggle not infrequently is between men in business and their wives and daughters'.

(Thomas Cubitt complaining of the fashionable world's preference for Belgravia over his developments in Bloomsbury)

Thomas Cubitt. (By courtesy of the National Portrait Gallery, London)

THOMAS Cubitt was born on 25 February 1788, the son of a Norfolk carpenter who was descended from farmers. When he died on 20 December 1855 Cubitt was one of the wealthiest men in England, a millionaire whose will, running to 386 pages, was the longest on record. He had built much of Victorian London. In Belgravia he had built fine dwellings for the titled, wealthy and fashionable elite of the world's largest metropolis. In Bloomsbury, Highbury and Pimlico he had built town houses for the aspiring middle classes. In Clapham he had built spacious villas for bankers and city merchants as well as a fine country home for himself. At Osborne, on the Isle of Wight, he had built a home for the Queen and her family, who had also asked him to extend and improve Buckingham Palace. Thomas Cubitt, at his death, had built more of London above ground than anyone else

Thomas Cubitt, at his death, had built more of London above ground than anyone else before or since

before or since. In the process he had devised novel methods of financing, managing and executing large contracts, which became the model for the future. What were the forces which created such a man?

The ship's carpenter

In about 1791 Thomas's parents moved from Norfolk to London in search of work for his father, the carpenter. Thomas, aged three, moved with them. The father died in 1806 leaving 18-year-old Thomas and two younger brothers, William and Lewis, both of whom worked with Thomas in the years ahead. At about the time of his father's death Thomas signed on as a carpenter for a ship bound for India. A ship's carpenter was a very important member of the crew and it was the custom, on some vessels, for the carpenter, as well as the captain and first mate, to receive a share of the profits of a voyage.[1] He returned to England and it may have been the rewards of the voyage that enabled him to take premises in Eagle Street, Holborn, and set up as a carpenter in 1810. His first major task was to re-roof the Russell Institution in nearby Great Coram Street. At this time the land of Thomas Coram's Foundling Hospital was being developed, to the great profit of the charity, and the Russell Institution had been built by the developer as a concert hall and assembly rooms for the occupants of his new dwellings. The original roofing had been found to be seriously defective and the glowing tributes that Thomas Cubitt earned from the Russell managers helped him to gain his first major building contract – the construction of the London Institution.

The London Institution

The London Institution had been founded in 1806 by a group of philanthropists 'for the Advancement of Literature and the Diffusion of Useful Knowledge'. Its principal asset was a fine library in Finsbury Circus, and an architect called William Brooks had been engaged to design a new building at Moorfields, nearby, to house the library and the Institution's other facilities. Tenders were invited for the construction work and in 1815 the contract, worth £20,000, was

View of the London Institution, Finsbury Circus, Thomas Cubitt's first major commission, 1820. (By courtesy of the Guildhall Library, Corporation of London)

awarded to Thomas Cubitt, harsh penalty clauses being inserted for late completion. This was an enormous contract by the standards of the time, equivalent to more than £20 *million* at 2002 prices, and its award to Thomas Cubitt is a testimony to the reputation that he had built in the five years that he had been in business.

In the early 19th century the conventional way for such a project to be executed was for the main contractor, in this case Cubitt, to sub-contract most of the work to smaller firms or self-employed individuals who could offer the necessary specialist skills. The problem with this arrangement was that the main contractor exercised little control over either the delivery of these services, or the quality of the work. Sub-contractors who had gained work through tendering very low prices might vanish in pursuit of more profitable work before or even during the execution of a contract that they had been awarded. Supervision was commonly inadequate or non-existent and probably helped to explain why the roofing on the Russell Institution had needed to be replaced within a few years of the building coming into use. In such conditions the chances of Thomas Cubitt completing a task as large as the construction of the London Institution on time, within budget and to the required standards were negligible.

New methods

For this reason Cubitt decided to adopt a different approach to the London Institution contract – a method that was to set a pattern for the future and which also helped to determine his future activity as a speculative house-builder. The word 'speculative' has come to have pejorative associations, but in this context it refers simply to the practice of building houses first and finding tenants afterwards rather than building to order. Cubitt took substantial premises on the east side of Grays Inn Road, where he employed the tradesmen he needed to execute the contract. They included bricklayers, masons, joiners, smiths, glaziers, slaters and paper-hangers. Key workers like foremen were provided with housing on the site, which remained in use until the 1960s. This was regarded at the time as a revolutionary and indeed risky method of doing business. In a tribute written after his death *The Builder* wrote of Cubitt's methods 'This bold and hazardous plan was then a novelty in London and consequently provoked much speculation'.[2] First, it could be more expensive because Cubitt would have to pay the going rate for the skills he needed and would not 'benefit' from the cost-cutting which could arise from the use of cheap sub-contractors executing shoddy work. His reply to this was that 'it is better to submit to paying rather more for the labour than to submit to the other evil of having it badly done'.[3] The second problem would

'This bold and hazardous plan was then a novelty in London'

arise when intervals occurred in Cubitt's contracting work. What would he do when he had no work for the men he was committed to employing? Would he lay them off and risk losing them or would he continue to pay them, with dire financial consequences? His answer to this was to employ them on the speculative building projects that created much of 19th century London. Finally, Cubitt committed himself to a substantial investment in premises and equipment which would not have been necessary if he had used sub-contractors.

Interior view of the pavilion erected on the premises of Messrs Cubitt, Gray's Inn Road, showing the anniversary banquet of the Conservative Association in 1837. It illustrates the scale of Cubitt's enterprise. (By courtesy of the Guildhall Library, Corporation of London)

The London Institution contract was finished on time in 1819 but it was not without its problems. Cubitt had great trouble with the architect, William Brooks, who frequently produced drawings and design details long after they were expected, obliging the frustrated Cubitt constantly to reschedule tasks so as to keep his workforce employed. It prompted Cubitt to declare that 'the best mode of proceeding with new buildings was to be independent of architects'. This experience may have contributed to Cubitt's lifelong aversion to the profession, which was just beginning to emerge as a discipline distinct from those of surveyor and builder. The Royal Institute of British Architects received its royal charter in 1837 but this was too long for Thomas Cubitt to wait. He assembled his own team of draughtsmen and surveyors at Grays Inn Road and took on his youngest brother Lewis[4] as an architect in his own employment over whom he could exercise full control. His younger brother, William, had already joined him in 1814. Later in life he made it clear that he did not wish to be thought of as an architect when the title was attached to him by a well-meaning journalist. He told the Select Committee on the State of Public Buildings 'I rather prefer being called a builder'.[5] The London Institution remained in Moorfields until 1936 when it was demolished.

'the best mode of proceeding with new buildings was to be independent of architects'

'Speculative building'

The London Institution contract brought Thomas Cubitt benefits in addition to the fee that he was paid for the work. The President of the Institution was Robert Smith, first Lord Carrington, of the influential banking firm of Smith, Payne and Smith, who in the years ahead was instrumental in securing finance for many of Cubitt's ventures. Another member of the Institution's governing body was J.W. Freshfield, founder of the law firm which bears his name. Freshfield was a Member of Parliament and a wealthy man who also invested in Cubitt's projects. It was to a friend of Freshfield's that Cubitt turned for the first of his speculative building ventures.

This friend was Lord Calthorpe, who owned land on the east side of Grays Inn Road stretching to the River Fleet, the present site of the Farringdon Road. At this time the area was largely rural, the fashionable spa of Bagnigge Wells being situated on what is now King's Cross Road. In November 1815, as work on the London Institution progressed fitfully under the constraints of William Brooks's untimely production of his drawings, Cubitt made an agreement with Lord Calthorpe. In return for the payment of ground rent on a small plot of land, Cubitt secured the right to build houses in what are now Frederick Street and Ampton Street. The streets were close to the site of Cubitt's workshop and thus ideally placed to occupy his workforce when they were waiting for the architect's drawings.

In September 1823 he took more ground from the Calthorpe estate to build what is now Cubitt Street, but in the meantime he had begun negotiations to buy land on the west side of Grays Inn Road reaching towards Bloomsbury. His first attempt was a failure. In 1819 he had tried to lease some land from the Foundling Hospital in the vicinity of what is now Mecklenburgh Square, but Cubitt, who always bargained hard, was unable to agree terms with the governors of the hospital. Instead he acquired some land in Highbury and a 12-acre plot in nearby Stoke Newington. In 1821, by Act of Parliament, Stoke Newington, along with other parts of London, had emerged from an archaic form of tenure known as copyhold, which survived from the Middle Ages. The occupants of such areas were technically still subject to the lord of the manor, which in their case was the dean and chapter of St Paul's Cathedral. Without their permission children could not inherit their parents' property. As these anomalies were removed by Acts of Parliament, areas like Stoke Newington became attractive to builders like Cubitt. Here he built 70 houses. Cubitt's investment by this time also included five acres of farmland in Barnsbury in the undeveloped area of Islington and 24 acres in nearby Copenhagen Fields, behind the present site of King's Cross Station. This area

The occupants of such areas were technically still subject to the lord of the manor

proved more difficult to develop. The small to medium-sized properties were hard to sell during the housing slump of the 1830s and the situation was made worse when the North London Railway was built through the development running east to west. The area south of the railway was eventually devoted to middle-class residences, while the land to the north bore smaller houses for clerks and artisans.

Bloomsbury: the beginnings

Cubitt now embarked on the first of his major developments on the Duke of Bedford's estate in Bloomsbury. Most of the land between the Covent Garden area and the Euston Road (then called the New Road) consisted of waterlogged fields. By the early 19th century the Covent Garden market, which had existed for over a century, had become surrounded by taverns, brothels and theatres, the employees of all three categories being regarded as almost equally undesirable as neighbours. Moreover, the purchase of Buckingham Palace by George III in 1762 had caused the centre of gravity of fashionable society to move west, so the few fine houses that existed in Bloomsbury had difficulty finding suitable tenants. People who could afford them did not want to live in the area and they decayed into tenements of the kind found in the notorious St Giles district close to where Tottenham Court Road underground station now stands. On the other hand Cubitt recognised that the clerks and tradesmen employed in the rapidly growing City of London required dwellings that were supplied with the more modest amenities appropriate to their station in life, and that were convenient for the City itself. In 1820, therefore, Cubitt took a 99-year lease on some land on the south side of Tavistock Square, at a peppercorn rent for the first five years and a rent of £200 per annum thereafter.

Cubitt built the houses in association with a stockbroker called Benjamin Oakley, who purchased them for £18,400 in March 1822. Cubitt completed the square in 1826, which, despite later bomb damage, retains some of the finest examples of his work.

Finance

Oakley was typical of the investors of the time, when opportunities for investments in secure assets were very limited. The Stock Exchange was still a rudimentary organisation and potential investors in the companies whose shares it offered were deterred by the prospect of unlimited liability. The passage of the Limited Liability Act in 1855 removed this obstacle but in the meantime joint stock companies were not an enticing prospect for the cautious investor. Purchase of a great landed estate, on the other hand, was beyond their means, and lending

taverns, brothels and theatres, the employees of all three categories being regarded as almost equally undesirable as neighbours

money to the Government, though a secure form of investment, offered low returns.

Investment in property, therefore, was attractive to investors with a few thousand or even a few hundred pounds available, though it was not without risk. In fashionable areas where tenants were easy to find an investment could be very profitable, but the sudden appearance of an undesirable amenity such as the North London Railway line in the midst of a development could turn a fashionable district into an undesirable one where tenancies were hard to fill. Cubitt enjoyed considerable success in attracting investors to his developments throughout his career. When his finances were stretched, as they often were in the early days, he sometimes sold out to investors at low prices. However, he did manage to remain solvent in a business which was notoriously cyclical and which claimed a number of eminent casualties.

Woburn Place, by Thomas Cubitt, is a place of charm and tranquillity in the heart of Bloomsbury.

Over the years that followed Cubitt continued to build dwellings for the aspiring middle classes on the Duke's estate. He built some charming town houses in Woburn Walk, off Upper Woburn Place, which have survived as a rare pedestrian area of small shops selling books, food and antiques, with dwellings above. Tavistock Square, Gordon Square and Woburn Place were developed mostly by Cubitt, together with most of the surrounding streets such as Endsleigh Street, Taviton Street and Torrington Place. On the south-west corner of Gordon Square the grandly named 'Cathedral and Metropolitan Church of the Catholic Apostolic Church' held its first service on Christmas Eve 1853. This curious foundation owed its origins to the

Catholic Apostolic
Church, Gordon
Square, whose massive
bulk caused the
collapse of Sir Morton
Peto's neighbouring
house.

Revd Edward Irving, a clergyman of Scottish extraction, who had preached three-hour sermons to huge congregations elsewhere in London, heard 'tongues' and became a persistent believer in the imminence of the Second Coming. Having been deprived of his living for heresy he set up the 'Catholic Apostolic Church', governed by a complicated hierarchy of 12 'apostles' and other dignitaries. He died in 1834 and the huge church in Gordon Square was built by his successor. Its construction caused the collapse of the neighbouring house, which belonged to Sir Samuel Morton Peto. Cubitt rebuilt Peto's house on the opposite corner, thereby ensuring that this prestigious tenant would remain in the square and, it was hoped, encourage other aspiring professionals to join him in the nearby dwellings. The church survives, now mostly converted to flats, an extravagant example of the Victorian 'mediaeval' style surrounded by Cubitt's classical designs.

SIR SAMUEL MORTON PETO, (1809–89)

Morton Peto was an apprentice bricklayer who inherited his uncle's building business and turned it into one of Britain's largest contractors. He built much of London clubland, including the Reform Club (to Charles Barry's design) and the Oxford and Cambridge Club in Pall Mall; parts of the Great Western, Great Eastern and South-Western railways; much of London's dockland; railways in Argentina, Australia, Russia, Canada, Algeria and Norway; part of the Palace of Westminster (again to Barry's design) and, most notably, Nelson's Column. He became a Member of Parliament in 1847 and his firm was one of many which failed in the financial crisis of 1866, following the collapse of the Overend Gurney bank.

'Building superior to anything which had been seen before'
Much of Cubitt's work has been destroyed by bombing or later development but enough remains for one authoritative writer to have described Cubitt's work in Bloomsbury as being of 'a style and quality superior to anything which had been seen before in the speculative market'[6] a judgement for which Cubitt must take most of the credit. However, some acknowledgement must also be made of the contri-

butions of the great estate owners upon whose land the dwellings were erected. At this time local government as we understand it was virtually non-existent. Such functions as were undertaken were discharged by vestries and paving boards, the latter bodies being established by individual Acts of Parliament to cover such matters as sanitation and the lighting, paving and cleaning of streets. In most cases their main aim was to keep down the rates payable by householders.

This matter was not resolved until the Metropolitan Board of Works took office in 1856[7] but in the meantime Cubitt took the precaution of securing his election to the paving board of the Calthorpe estate in 1820, when he was building in the area, and was a strong advocate of installing adequate sewers in all his developments. In the absence of any recognisable planning authority the size, design and appearance of buildings was a matter for negotiation between the builder, the prospective tenants and the landlord, or, more often, the landlord's agent. Each estate owner would have his own views on the desirability of different types of tenant. Everyone agreed that brewers, smiths and soap-makers were undesirable because of the noise and smell they created, but a complacent landlord could deposit one of these unwanted neighbours in any area he chose. Most agreed that shops made a development attractive but butchers were particularly unpopular if they had their own slaughter-houses, since these notoriously generated the most undesirable waste. In this respect Cubitt was fortunate, since the Duke of Bedford appears to have been an enlightened landlord. The Duke, however, did insist that pavements on his estate be constructed of Yorkshire stone, while carriageways were to be of granite – a requirement which ensured that deafening noise would be a characteristic of the area until the streets were covered with conventional tarmacadam a century later.

Cubitt and the Duke's steward, Christopher Haedy, corresponded on the difficulties of finding suitable tenants as the number of dwellings expanded. As already indicated[8] fashionable society had migrated to the west and in 1840 Cubitt wrote to Haedy:

> 'The great struggle not infrequently is between men in business and their wives and daughters. Their convenience would keep them here within easy reach of their places of business, but their wives and daughters would give their preference to a more fashionable address at the western or north-western end of this town'.[9]

He was referring to the growth of Belgravia, in which he was himself involved, and two years later he wrote in starker terms: 'The fact is the

carriageways were to be of granite – a requirement which ensured that deafening noise would be a characteristic of the area

place is become unfashionable. Everybody is running away to the West'.

In the meantime a number of expedients were adopted to help fill the vacant buildings that were arising in Bloomsbury. The agent was alarmed when Cubitt proposed that three vacant dwellings in Gordon Square should be converted into a 'seminary' – a euphemism for a student hostel. After some discussion this proposal was accepted in the absence of any better offers and the building next to the 'Metropolitan Church' became Coward College, a centre for training Dissenting clergymen, which became part of London University in 1900.

Belgravia

One of the reasons for Cubitt's over-stretched finances lay in the fashionable area to the west that was proving so attractive to the wives and daughters of City businessmen. The name 'Belgravia' was attached to the area south of Hyde Park by its owners the Grosvenor family, earls and later dukes of Westminster. The name came from one of the family's estates to the north of Leicester, called Belgrave, but its foreign-sounding name continued to deceive for many years. *The Builder* reported that a letter addressed to 'Thomas Cubitt, Belgravia' had been sent by the Post Office to Vienna.[10] Its location, close to Buckingham Palace, was in its favour, but in other respects it was not an attractive residential area. Much of it was below high-water mark and liable to flooding when tides were high. The King's Scholars' Pond sewer and the Ranelagh sewer flowed through it and by 1820 they were filled with London's sewage. The area contained many market gardens supplying vegetables like tomatoes and asparagus to the market in Covent Garden, so there was no shortage of wheeled traffic along its dusty roads, the most important being the Kings Road, which, until 1831, was for the exclusive use of the monarch. The area also contained one of London's largest rubbish dumps. The most prominent buildings were St George's Hospital (now the Lanesborough Hotel) and Tattershall's auction rooms where racehorses were traded. Both of these were close to the present site of Hyde Park Corner and adjacent to Tattershall's was a field in which horses awaiting the auctioneer's hammer were tethered. In 1820 the construction of the Grosvenor Canal to the south of the area led to the growth of a small industrial estate, which included the works of Bramah and Hunter, manufacturers of the newly fashionable water-closets. Soon the premises of Thomas Cubitt himself would join them.

Given the rather unpromising nature of the area it says much for Cubitt's prescience that, in the words of a tribute in *The Builder* 'Perceiving the disposition of the fashionable world to follow in the

the Kings Road, which, until 1831, was for the exclusive use of the monarch

wake of royalty, Mr Cubitt fixed on a tract of land for big speculations at the nearest place he could find in the vicinity of the royal palace'.[11] In 1824 he leased 19 acres from the Grosvenor estate. He was to pay £6 an acre for the first six years, while the development was under way, rising in steps to £150 an acre after 12 years. Cubitt eventually developed 140 acres of the Grosvenor estate in this part of London.

View of Belgrave Square's north east side, 1828. (By courtesy of the Guildhall Library, Corporation of London)

Before he could begin to build houses he had first to establish the infrastructure. He spent £9,000 enlarging, strengthening and re-routing the Ranelagh sewer. He paved and lit the roads. Then he began to build, starting with Belgrave Square, the principal architect being George Basevi, cousin to Benjamin Disraeli. The style is neo-classical, terraces of brick with stucco, which became the hallmark of the Belgravia development. The first house, completed in 1828, was occupied by Henry Drummond of the prominent banking family. Such tenants were essential if other suitably affluent and well-connected occupants were to be attracted to the area. Another early resident was the Earl of Essex, popularly referred to at the time as 'the decoy duck' because of his famed ability to attract other fashionable tenants. The great coup, however, came in 1840, when Queen Victoria took a house in the square for her troublesome mother the Duchess of Kent. The Duchess was neither a popular nor a pleasant lady, but the royal connection thus firmly established ensured that other members of fashionable society quickly followed. Thomas Kemp, the developer of Kemptown in Brighton who had sold the site of the Brighton Pavilion to Queen Victoria's uncle, the Prince Regent, took one of the splendid villas on the corner of the square. Another, in the north-east corner of the square, was taken by Sidney Herbert, the much put-upon supporter of Florence Nightingale who made preparations for her

Crimean venture in the house. Lord John Russell, later Prime Minister, took a house in nearby Chesham Place in 1840. Belgrave Square was swiftly followed by Eaton Square, where many of the houses were again designed by Basevi. The first house in Eaton Square was taken in 1827 by the brewer W.H. Whitbread, though he later 'part-exchanged' it for a larger one nearby. Smaller houses on Eaton Terrace changed hands for £1,700, while those closer to the Kings Road commanded prices of up to £4,000. Houses in Eaton Square itself cost £7,000.[12] The area came to be referred to for a while as 'Cubittopolis'. Pevsner calls it 'the crowning achievement of Thomas Cubitt'.[13]

View of Eaton Square, showing buildings under construction, in the heart of 'Cubittopolis', 1827. (By courtesy of the Guildhall Library, Corporation of London)

THOMAS KEMP (1782–1844)

Thomas Kemp was born in Lewes Castle in 1782, the son of a wealthy landowner. He acquired a second fortune when he married into the Baring banking family. He served briefly as a rather inactive MP for Lewes, during which time he formed a Dissenting sect. In 1816 he left Parliament and built a chapel for the new sect, briefly serving there as a minister. He also built a temple, supposedly on the dimensions of Solomon's temple, which later served as a girls' school. Kemp owned a large area of land to the east of Brighton between the seafront and the racecourse and in the 1820s he began to build 'Kemptown', a vast estate of over a hundred houses for the gentry. Some of them were built by Thomas Cubitt. The scheme swallowed up his own fortune and those of his first and second wives. He had re-entered Parliament in 1823, but his financial condition continued to deteriorate and his fortune diminished as Kemptown grew. In 1837 he left Parliament again and went to live in Paris. A few months before his death in 1844 he was declared bankrupt and a notice to that effect was nailed to the door of St Nicholas Church, Brighton.

'Malta' and 'Gibraltar'

Cubitt now moved on to the neighbouring Lowndes estate in the area named after the bridge over the Westbourne River – the Knights' Bridge. He leased a workshop on the northern side of what is now Lowndes Square and proceeded to develop the area, beginning with Pont Street and William Street and moving on to Halkin Terrace and Lowndes Square itself, where the houses were designed by Cubitt's youngest brother Lewis. He now undertook one of his more controversial ventures. For some years the Government had been sympathetic to the idea of improving the southern aspect of Hyde Park without wishing to spend any money on it. This was the point at which the River Westbourne left the park on its journey from its source in Hampstead to the Thames, surfacing briefly in Hyde Park as the Serpentine[14]. By 1840 the Westbourne was an open sewer, conveying much of London's sewage to the polluted Thames, a condition in which it was to remain until the main drainage works of Sir Joseph Bazalgette 25 years later.[15] The exit from the park was further marred by the presence of a brewery called 'The Cannon', which had chosen the site because of its proximity to the Westbourne and its ready supply of water (mixed, by 1840, with sewage). The Government's wish to give greater dignity to this exit from the royal park coincided with Cubitt's wish to create a grand entrance to his developments in Belgravia and Knightsbridge. The brewery was bought by Cubitt and demolished, the Westbourne was covered over and Albert Gate was thereby created. On either side of the gate Cubitt built two huge houses of a height so much greater than the surrounding buildings that for the first time he employed a hoist rather than ladders to take his men to the upper storeys of the building while the work was in progress. The buildings were derisively named by the press 'Malta' and Gibraltar' on the grounds that, like those two great Mediterranean fortresses, 'they would never be taken' but the critics were wrong. In 1846 one was taken by the great railway entrepreneur George Hudson, then at the height of his power. He paid £13,667 and when his railway empire collapsed the following year the house was taken by the French ambassador. It remains the French embassy. The other house is now the embassy of Kuwait.

Not everyone was impressed by Cubitt's work. Disraeli declared that Belgravia was 'as monstrous as Marylebone and so contrived as to be at the same time insipid and tawdry'. Nevertheless, despite the

'Malta' and 'Gibraltar', Cubitt's two houses at Albert Gate; so massive for their age. They now house the French and Kuwaiti embassies.

The buildings were derisively named by the press 'Malta' and 'Gibraltar' on the grounds that, like those two great Mediterranean fortresses, 'they would never be taken'

Disraeli declared that Belgravia was 'as monstrous as Marylebone and so contrived as to be at the same time insipid and tawdry'

great Conservative's strictures Belgravia remains one of London's most fashionable areas, though very few can now afford to live there. In May 2002 the terraced house at 5, Belgrave Square, with its seven reception rooms, seven bedrooms and private cinema, went on sale for £25 million. It is the former home of the Conservative MP and socialite Sir Henry 'Chips' Channon. At the time he purchased it in 1935 Channon, who married into the Guinness family, described it as 'dirt-cheap compared with all the other houses we have seen but we will make it gay and comfortable'. It is one of the few private residences left in the square, which has become the heart of London's diplomatic quarter, with embassies on every side. The first was that of Austria, which entered Belgrave Square in the 19th century, and the square itself now accommodates more than a dozen diplomatic missions.

No.5, Belgrave Square, Chips Channon's former home, built by Thomas Cubitt, a bargain at £25 million.

Pimlico

Cubitt now moved south on to a further stretch of the Grosvenor estate in the area known as 'Neathouses', but better known as Pimlico. In the early 19th century the area was even more susceptible to flooding than Belgravia, much of it given over to market gardens growing asparagus, tomatoes and liquorice, whose proprietors were most reluctant to give up their land. Nevertheless, by 1827 Cubitt had leased 85 acres from the Grosvenor estate. This was a much more difficult area to develop than any he had yet faced. A century and a half later, when building the Victoria Line, 20th-century engineers encountered major difficulties tunnelling through the waterlogged ground. Cubitt imported 180,000 cubic yards of spoil to raise the ground level, much of it brought by barge from St Katherine's Dock, which was being constructed at the time. He also enlarged and strengthened the King's Scholars' Pond sewer, which flowed through the area after passing beneath Buckingham Palace. He was not allowed to cover it over, as he wished, because the authorities feared that, at high tides, sewage might back up into the sewer and emerge in the cellars of Buckingham Palace. It was thought more decorous for it to overflow into the houses of Pimlico until the restriction was lifted in 1844. Cubitt also fought a rearguard action against the Great Western Railway, which wanted to build its terminus at Bessborough Gardens, close to the river. With the enthusiastic support of other landowners he saw off this threat. Isambard Kingdom Brunel and the Great Western settled for Paddington.

sewage might back up into the sewer and emerge in the cellars of Buckingham Palace

The development of Pimlico followed a different pattern from that of Belgravia. Its proximity to the stinking Thames and its distance from the residences of the fashionable made it an area for artisans and clerks rather than aristocrats, and this distinction was reflected both in the more modest character of the residences and in its other amenities. In Belgravia Cubitt confined public houses to the mews where servants lived, judging that the titled inhabitants would be more comfortable in the drawing room than the saloon bar. In Pimlico leases for pubs were much more common and were often the first to be granted in a designated area. This was common practice in other parts of London, though unusual for Cubitt, who disapproved of strong drink. Because of the profits they could generate, pubs could command five times the rent of a dwelling, though there could be problems obtaining a licence from the magistrates. *The Builder* explained the attraction of pubs for developers in 1854:[16]

Whereas a nice Cubitt home in Pimlico can be yours for less than a million.

> 'One speculative builder, reserving all the angle-plots, [i.e. corner sites] *runs up half a dozen public houses: he obtains licences for all that he can, and lets or sells such at incredible prices or enormous rentals; others he sells to adventuring publicans who try for the privilege* [i.e. the licence] *or, in the case of failure, open as Beer-shops at war with the bench'*.

The area was not fully developed until the 1870s, two decades after Cubitt's death, but by 1845 *The Builder* could comment that 'Pimlico, from being heretofore little better than a swamp, now promises to become one of the most splendid and luxurious quarters of the neighbourhood'. It wasn't quite splendid enough for Anthony Trollope's Lady Alexandrina in *The Small House at Allington*, however, who narrowly escaped beginning her married life in Pimlico when warned of the modest character of the area by a well-meaning friend: 'If indeed they could have achieved Eaton Square ... Her geographical knowledge of Pimlico had not been perfect and she had very nearly fallen into a fatal error'. A narrow escape indeed from social perdition!

The development of Pimlico varied in another

Pimlico 'angle plot' pub; loyally named after the landowner, such pubs made the area attractive to investors.

way from that of Cubitt's other projects in that much of the work was undertaken by small builders who took sites from Cubitt and often bought their materials from him as well. By this time Cubitt, as well as being London's biggest builder, was also a major supplier of building materials.

The workshop

The original workshop off Grays Inn Road had passed out of Cubitt's hands in 1827 when his brother William took it over as part of a separate contracting business, leaving Thomas to concentrate on speculative building. By 1828 Thomas was employing 1,000 men in Belgravia alone and the workshop that he had created in Lowndes Square was no longer adequate for his needs. In 1839 therefore he began to build a new workshop on the banks of the Thames, west of the present site of Vauxhall Bridge. Much of the site was later occupied by the fashionable residence of Dolphin Square. On this huge site, covering about 50 acres, Cubitt built a workshop and storage area which was to supply his developments in Belgravia and Pimlico. He embanked 3,000 feet of the river frontage so that his own fleet of specially constructed barges could be used to bring in timber, cement, sand, gravel and other raw materials. A brickworks was built to convert the unstable clay excavated from the subsoil of Belgravia into bricks for the houses he was building there. A steam engine was installed to supply power for forges and lathes. A testing facility was built where girders, bricks and other components were tested to destruction before the batches of which they were part could be used on his construction projects. The workshop also acted as a storage depot from which materials like bricks and cement were supplied on credit to the smaller builders who were developing Pimlico.

George Godwin, founding editor of *The Builder*, gave an account of the works which was published in 1845 and shows Cubitt to have been an enlightened employer.[17] The writer found well-lit, heated workrooms with cooking and drying facilities, water-closets and subsidised coffee and cocoa to discourage the consumption of strong drink. There was a reading room with newspapers and a lending library, this being nine years before the first public lending library was opened in London. Evening lectures were given for apprentices. The working week was also slightly shorter at Cubitt's workshop. Every day began at 6am, but on Saturdays Cubitt's men finished at 4, not 6pm. *The Builder*, in its distinctly flattering assessment, declared that 'The best workmen are anxious to be employed there; a drunken man is unknown in the establishment'. The most important people in the workshop were the foremen, many of whom had started with Cubitt

'The best workmen are anxious to be employed there; a drunken man is unknown in the establishment'

as apprentices and were critical to his quality assurance regime. They visited sites to ensure that the right materials were being used and that designs were being executed in the correct manner and with the materials specified. Some of them went on to greater things. George Dines, for example, the general foreman in charge of the works, went on to build the Frogmore Mausoleum for Queen Victoria in 1871.

In his obituary in *The Builder* Cubitt was quoted as saying that 'If you wait until people thank you for doing anything for them, you will never do anything; it is right for me to do it, whether they are thankful for it or not'.[18] There speaks the Victorian patriarch, but his benevolent paternalism was put to the test on 17 August 1854 when a disastrous fire destroyed much of the workshop. It was a great event reported not just in trade magazines like *The Builder,* but also in *The Times* and the *Illustrated London News.* The new floor which had been made for the ballroom at Buckingham Palace was consumed, together with another floor that was ready to be laid in a drawing room at Windsor Castle. Estimates of the value of the damage reached £100,000, of which Cubitt recovered a little over £6,000 from insurers. Among the casualties were the tools of the workmen he employed. The morning after the fire he announced 'Tell the men they shall be at work within a week and I will subscribe £600 towards buying them new tools'.[19] He was as good as his word. Within a month the men had recovered 80 percent of the cost of their tools and the joiners submitted a written testimonial which was published in *The Builder,* in which declared that they 'cannot but feel that he has in this present instance offered a still greater manifestation of his generous spirit towards his workmen'.[20]

In July 1851 Cubitt purchased 17 acres of land at Aylesford on the River Medway in Kent, an area well supplied with the clay and chalk that were required to make bricks and cement. There he installed a brickworks which made use of the latest machinery and techniques, including a brickmaking machine patented 10 years earlier, and rail connections between the claypits, machinery, kilns and drying racks. The new site cost him £54,000 and became the principal supplier of bricks to his own works as well as to those of other builders as the railway building boom gathered pace.

By Royal Command

In 1844 Cubitt became involved in the task of creating a suitable country residence for the royal family. Brighton Pavilion, the exotic creation of the Prince Regent, later George IV, was felt by Victoria and Albert to be unsuitable as a family residence on account of its association with the louche lifestyle of her late uncle. In August 1844

'Tell the men they shall be at work within a week and I will subscribe £600 towards buying them new tools'

the royal couple visited Osborne House on the Isle of Wight. Victoria was enthusiastic about the site and the more serious Albert was impressed by the opportunities it presented of introducing 'improving' agricultural schemes. It is not clear why Cubitt was approached as the preferred builder, though his contact with the family through the lease of the house in Belgrave Square to the Queen's mother may have had some influence. Albert was given a conducted tour of Cubitt's Pimlico workshop and was taken to see 'Malta' and 'Gibraltar' at the entrance to Hyde Park. He was evidently as impressed by Cubitt's workshop as the editor of *The Builder* had been and equally struck by 'Malta' and 'Gibraltar', since the architectural style adopted for Osborne resembled those two maligned buildings. Cubitt spent almost five years working on the Osborne project, his draughtsmen being used to create drawings to Albert's exacting specifications. The two men appear to have enjoyed an excellent relationship and this probably explains the high opinion that Victoria came to hold of the builder whom she came to refer to as 'our Mr Cubitt'.

On 1 March 1846 Cubitt took the Queen and the Prince on a tour of the work in progress and Victoria delightedly recorded in her journal: 'The staircase and ceiling are in and it will be quite delightful. I can hardly believe we shall be living in this charming house, built by ourselves, in a few months'. The 'built by ourselves' may be taken as proprietary pride rather than an undervaluing of Cubitt's contribution, since six months later, on 14 September, she wrote again: 'All is very convenient, spacious and well carried out. Mr Cubitt has done it admirably. He is such an honest, kind, good man'. Once the family had moved in, Cubitt's staff continued to maintain and clean the house until the royal household was fully established. In a society so concerned with protocol this must have been a delicate matter, and it is a testimony to Cubitt's management that the task was accomplished without any rupture in relations between himself and the sensitive Queen.

Cubitt now moved on to Buckingham Palace itself, which at the time was almost uninhabitable. George IV, dissatisfied, as he usually was, with anything connected with his late father, had decided that the palace bought by George III in 1762 was quite unsuitable as the London home of a prince as magnificent as himself. By the time of his death he had spent over £500,000 of taxpayers' money demolishing and embellishing the palace, and had succeeded in convincing Parliament that he should not be given further access to the public purse.[21] The most enduring evidence of his ambition lay in the form of the Marble Arch, the huge edifice designed and erected by John Nash in 1828 to give a suitably awe-inspiring entrance to the palace.

A new east front for the palace and two wings were designed by an architect called Edward Blore and Cubitt was awarded the building contract in 1846 on unusually favourable terms. It was normal procedure for such Government contracts to be put out to tender, but Cubitt explained 'I cannot enter into competition with other Tradesmen as to prices'. This condition was accepted, Cubitt himself being awarded the whole building contract. It was eventually executed for a little over £100,000, well within the sum voted by Parliament. Moreover, Cubitt had also helped to negotiate the sale of the Brighton Pavilion to the town of Brighton for £53,000, offsetting half the cost of the work at the palace. There were problems, however, especially for the architect Edward Blore. He was subjected to constant interference over design details by well-meaning courtiers and was persuaded to use Caen stone to face the palace despite his own doubts about its durability. Within 10 years the façade was crumbling and the problem was not solved until the building was refaced in 1913 by Sir Aston Webb.

There remained the question of what to do with Nash's Marble Arch, which was now awkwardly situated a few feet from the new east front of the palace like a huge and ungainly front porch. In August

View of Buckingham House in 1754 before its transformation into Buckingham Palace. (By courtesy of the Guildhall Library, Corporation of London)

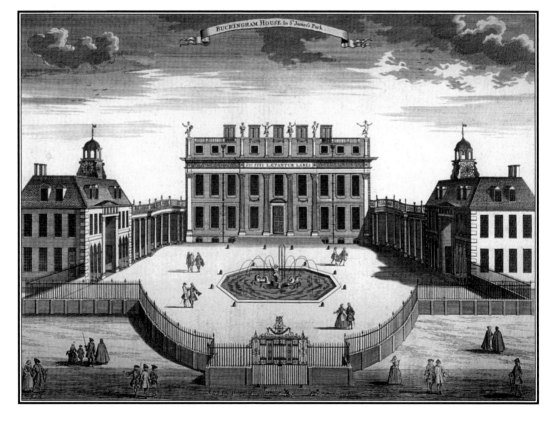

View of Queen Victoria returning from the House of Lords, showing the front of Buckingham Palace, with the Marble Arch in its original position, 1839. (By courtesy of the Guildhall Library, Corporation of London)

1850 Cubitt dismantled the arch and deposited it stone by stone in St James's Park, each piece being numbered so that it could be reassembled when a new home was found. This took several months, but eventually it was re-erected on its present site, as an entrance to Hyde Park, in time for the Great Exhibition of 1851.

A wider world

Thomas Cubitt is mostly remembered for his work in building much of 19th-century London, but his benign influence extended to other spheres. He was a strong campaigner for better sanitation. It has already been observed that he took care to ensure that all his dwellings were provided with well-constructed sewers, and he was an early advocate of a comprehensive system of main drainage of the kind that was eventually constructed by Sir Joseph Bazalgette after Cubitt's death.[22] He was also one of the first campaigners for a smoke-free atmosphere in London and argued for the widespread adoption of engines and furnaces that consumed their own smoke, one of which he installed in his workshops at Grays Inn Road and Pimlico. He argued that the extra cost 'would be fully compensated by the advantage they would receive' in cleaner clothing, furniture and buildings. He fell into a dispute with Colonel Samuel Colt, who had rented part of Cubitt's premises at Pimlico to make his revolvers, because Colt had a smoking chimney. Cubitt publicly advocated the purchase of agricultural land close to the centre of the metropolis as public open spaces, fearing that developers would drive the prices up to a point where they would be beyond the public purse. It was as a result of his campaigning that Battersea Park was purchased and opened in 1853. He also suggested that the embankment he had built at his works in Pimlico should be extended westwards through Chelsea, but another 20 years passed before this scheme was realised by Sir Joseph Bazalgette in 1874.

Thomas Cubitt must also take some of the credit for the Great Exhibition of 1851 and its aftermath. In June 1849 he had a conversation with a friend, Francis Fuller, about a visit that Fuller had made to an exhibition in Paris. On 14 June, during a visit to Osborne, Cubitt passed on the content of the conversation to Prince Albert, and two weeks later Albert called a meeting of Cubitt, Fuller, John Scott Russell and Henry Cole, at which the five men formulated the idea of the world's first 'Exhibition of all Nations', at which all nationalities would be invited to exhibit.[23] Thereafter the work of organising the exhibition was driven mostly by the energy of Henry Cole, though Cubitt did act as a guarantor of £5,000 of the sum advanced by the Bank of England to mount the exhibition. Thomas Cubitt's guarantee was not called upon since the Great Exhibition, attended by six million people, generated a surplus of £186,000. Albert wanted to use this money to purchase land south of Hyde Park in Kensington to accommodate the National Gallery and other suitable educational and cultural institutions. He especially requested Thomas Cubitt to undertake the delicate negotiations for the purchase of the land, which involved an awkward Frenchman called Baron de Villars who owned 48 acres. After some long and hard bargaining Cubitt agreed a price of £150,000 and the site passed to the Commissioners of the Great Exhibition. The National Gallery preferred to remain in Trafalgar Square but, in the decades that followed, the Kensington site became the home of the Royal Albert Hall, the Imperial College of Science and Technology and the many museums with which the area is associated.[24]

'That excellent and worthy man'

Cubitt never retired, many of his developments remaining unfinished at his death, but in 1851 he built a fine country home for himself called Denbies, near Dorking in Surrey. In choosing this location he may have been influenced by his experience of the area in the 1820s

He fell into a dispute with Colonel Samuel Colt, who had rented part of Cubitt's premises at Pimlico to make his revolvers

when he rebuilt the nearby Polesden Lacey house for a bookseller who had bought it in a decrepit state from the estate of the playwright Richard Sheridan. Prior to that date he had lived for 19 years in a mansion which he had built for himself at Clapham Park, on the south side of Clapham Common. This was still a rural area to the south of London, which was the home of the Clapham Sect, including fellow philanthropists like William Wilberforce and the banking family of Thornton, whom he knew as friends. There he was waited on by 12 servants and surrounded by a fine garden of 22 acres. On the surrounding area, amounting to over 200 acres, he built large, detached country villas for wealthy bankers and merchants. He continued to use it as his London home after he moved to Dorking, where he died on 20 December 1855, leaving eleven children. The Queen recorded in her journal on Christmas Eve that she was 'much grieved by the death of that excellent and worthy man Mr Thomas Cubitt ... he is a real national loss. A better, kinderhearted or more simple, unassuming man never breathed'. His obituary reminded its readers of his human qualities: 'to those under him, and holding responsible situations, he was generous and kind, blending his position as master with that of a friend'.[25] Cubitt's eldest son, George, inherited the business and in 1892 became the first Lord Ashcombe. Denbies was demolished in 1953 and a smaller house of the same name built on the site. In 2000 a memorial statue to Thomas Cubitt was unveiled at Ranmore, Dorking, close to his former home.

Thomas Cubitt's company survived and eventually merged with others to form Holland, Hannen and Cubitts, the Cubitt family being involved in both its ownership and management. Thomas Cubitt is commemorated by a street named in his honour in Holborn and by the Cubitt Room at 1, Queen Anne's Gate, St James's Park, where Holland, Hannen and Cubitts established their headquarters in the 1920s. Thomas Cubitt is unknown to most of the people who live in his houses, walk through his streets or admire the fine buildings he created in Bloomsbury, Belgravia and elsewhere. Yet they remain the most enduring monument to his memory, together with the construction methods that he pioneered and which quickly became the model for the great engineering companies of the late 19th and 20th centuries. Perhaps his epitaph should be the quotation from John Ruskin that is to be found on the statue of Sir Robert Grosvenor, ancestor of the Duke of Westminster, at the junction of Belgrave Square and Wilton Crescent:

'When we build let us think we build for ever'.

A better, kinderhearted or more simple, unassuming man never breathed

[1] *Selkirk's Island*, Diana Souhami, Phoenix, 2001, page 118.

[2] *The Builder*, 9 February 1856, page 72 'The late Mr Cubitt'.

[3] Select Committee on the State of Public Buildings, page 406.

[4] Lewis Cubitt was the architect who later designed King's Cross Station.

[5] Select Committee on the State of Public Buildings, page 407.

[6] J. Summerson: *Georgian London*, Barrie & Jenkins, 1988, page 181.

[7] See Chapter 6 for an account of the works of the Board.

[8] See page 57 above.

[9] *Town Planning in London: the eighteenth and nineteenth centuries*, D. Olsen, Yale, 1964, page 111.

[10] *The Builder*, 15 November 1873, page 898; an old story: Cubitt had died 18 years earlier.

[11] *The Builder*, 9 February 1856, page 72 'The late Mr Cubitt'.

[12] It is notoriously hard to equate prices with modern values but a multiplier of 1,000 will give a fair idea of present day values. So £7,000 in the early 19th century would be about £7 million in 2002.

[13] *The Buildings of England*, Kensington and Chelsea, Penguin, 1978.

[14] The Westbourne may also be seen at Sloane Square underground station in a culvert which runs across the station above the trains.

[15] See Chapter 6 for an account of these works.

[16] *The Builder*, 25 February 1854, page 96.

[17] *The Builder*, 1 February 1845, page 49.

[18] *The Builder*, 29 December 1855, page 629, Cubitt's obituary notice.

[19] *The Builder*, 29 December 1855, page 629, Cubitt's obituary notice.

[20] *The Builder*, 23 September 1854, page 467.

[21] See Chapter 1 for an account of George IV's financial troubles over the palace.

[22] See Chapter 6 for an account of Bazalgette's work.

[23] See Chapter 4 for an account of the Great Exhibition and the Crystal Palace.

[24] See Chapter 8 for an account of the building of the Natural History Museum.

[25] *Minutes of Proceedings, Institution of Civil Engineers*, vol. xvi, 1856–7, page 162.

CHAPTER 4

Sir Joseph Paxton and the Great Exhibition

'He rose from the ranks to be the greatest gardener of his time, the founder of a new style of architecture, and a man of genius, who devoted it to objects in the highest and noblest sense popular'.
(*The Times*, 9 June 1865, in its obituary of Sir Joseph Paxton, creator of the Crystal Palace)

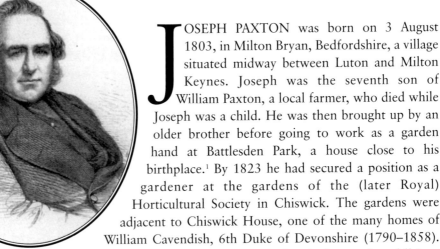

Joseph Paxton.
(*Illustrated London News*)

JOSEPH PAXTON was born on 3 August 1803, in Milton Bryan, Bedfordshire, a village situated midway between Luton and Milton Keynes. Joseph was the seventh son of William Paxton, a local farmer, who died while Joseph was a child. He was then brought up by an older brother before going to work as a garden hand at Battlesden Park, a house close to his birthplace.[1] By 1823 he had secured a position as a gardener at the gardens of the (later Royal) Horticultural Society in Chiswick. The gardens were adjacent to Chiswick House, one of the many homes of William Cavendish, 6th Duke of Devonshire (1790–1858). The Duke, who had an interest in horticulture, often fell into conversation with the young man as he walked through the Society's grounds and was sufficiently impressed by Joseph's lively intelligence to offer him the post of head gardener at the Duke's principal residence, the 17th-century mansion Chatsworth House, near Chesterfield, in Derbyshire. Paxton later wrote an account of his arrival at Chatsworth:

> 'I left London by the Comet *coach for Chesterfield;
> arrived at Chesterfield at 4.30 in the morning of the*

ninth of May, 1826. As no person was to be seen at that early hour I got over the greenhouse gate by the old covered way, explored the pleasure gardens and looked round the outside of the house. I then went down to the kitchen gardens, scaled the outside wall and saw the whole of the place, set the men to work there at six o'clock; then returned to Chesterfield and got Thomas Weldon to play me the waterworks and afterwards went to breakfast with poor dear Mrs Gregory and her niece. The latter fell in love with me and I with her, and thus completed my first morning's work at Chatsworth before nine o'clock.'

The latter fell in love with me and I with her, and thus completed my first morning's work at Chatsworth before nine o'clock.

The briskness of the account, written towards the end of his career, may owe something to hindsight, but it conveys the energy and decisiveness which were to characterise all his future enterprises. The niece, Sarah Brown, was from a prosperous family long established in the area. She became Mrs Joseph Paxton in January 1827, eight months after the first meeting, and brought with her a substantial dowry of £5,000: more than useful to a man whose salary upon appointment was £70 a year. She remained attached to Chatsworth throughout her life and was constantly drawn back there long after the centre of her husband's interests had moved to London, a place where she never felt quite comfortable.

A gardener of distinction

Joseph Paxton's association with the Crystal Palace has obscured the fact that, in his early career, he was a gardener of distinction with a number of achievements to his credit. In 1840 he co-authored a *Pocket Botanical Dictionary* with John Lindley (1799–1865), a Fellow of the Royal Society and professor of botany at the University of London. However, his most notable achievement in this early phase of his career was in the propagation of a dwarf banana which had been found in Mauritius and defied all previous attempts to cultivate it. Paxton succeeded in propagating it at Chatsworth and was responsible for its introduction to Samoa, where it remains a staple food item. For his success the Horticultural Society awarded him a silver medal. His growing reputation was further recognised two years later, in 1838, when he was one of three people appointed to survey the botanical gardens at Kew, an event which brought him into contact with Sir William Hooker (1785–1865) director of the gardens. Sir William was to prove a very useful contact in one of Paxton's most remarkable successes eight years later.

SIR WILLIAM HOOKER (1785–1865)

William Hooker was born at Norwich in 1785 and inherited a considerable estate at the age of four. He was interested in natural history from childhood and became acquainted with Sir Joseph Banks, who had accompanied Captain James Cook in *The Endeavour* on his first historic journey to Australia. Hooker became professor of botany at Glasgow University. He was a fine teacher, established the university's botanic garden and would probably have remained in Glasgow had he not been offered the opportunity to become the first director of the Royal Botanic Gardens at Kew. The gardens had fallen into a poor condition since the death of George III and some of the glasshouses stocked with rare plants narrowly avoided being converted into vineyards to supply the royal table. Hooker became director in 1841 and built up both the collection and the buildings, commissioning the famous palm house from Decimus Burton.[2] Hooker was a friend and admirer of Joseph Paxton, to whom he supplied the famous *Victoria regia* lily. This led Paxton to design the celebrated lily house which formed the inspiration for the Crystal Palace. When Hooker died in 1865 Kew was unrivalled as a centre for the study of botany. His son, Joseph Hooker, was also a famous botanist and friend of Charles Darwin.

First steps in building design

In the meantime Joseph Paxton was becoming involved in the field in which he was to make his lasting reputation: the design of buildings. In 1838 the Duke decided that the nearby village of Edensor should be moved so that it should not disturb the view from the recently extended Chatsworth. Joseph Paxton was given the task of organising the rebuilding of the village on its present site. At this time he also designed Prince's Park in Liverpool, a commission which he undertook in conjunction with the architect to the Commissioners of Woods and Forests. This architect was James Pennethorne (1801–71), adopted son of John Nash,[3] so it is not surprising that the designs for Prince's Park were similar in many respects to those of Regent's Park, London.

The missing emperor

Chatsworth received many royal visitors during Joseph Paxton's time and the Duke entrusted his gardener with the organisation of pageants and other entertainments to divert their royal highnesses. On one occasion, in 1843, the Queen and Prince Albert were accompanied by the Duke of Wellington, who was much impressed by the tidy state of the grounds on the morning after the previous evening's festivities. Upon enquiry he learned that Paxton had been up for much of the night with a hundred workmen, clearing away the debris, which prompted Wellington to tell the Duke of Devonshire 'I should have liked that man of yours for one of my generals'. The following year, 1844, plans were made for a visit of Tsar Nicholas I of Russia, a friend of the Duke, and Paxton suggested that, in honour of the visit, it would be appropriate to complete the work on a great fountain which he had already begun. To create an eight-acre reservoir 100,000 cubic feet of earth were moved, to supply a fountain which threw its water almost 300 feet into the air – the greatest height ever reached by a fountain. The fountain survives as perhaps the most spectacular monument to Sir Joseph Paxton, but there was one disappointment: the Tsar did not go to Chatsworth during his visit to England and thus never saw the great fountain which had been named the Emperor Fountain in his honour.

'I should have liked that man of yours for one of my generals'

The 'Great Stove'

In the early 1830s Paxton had begun to experiment with different designs for glasshouses, or conservatories. He was seeking a design

Paxton's 'Great Stove' at Chatsworth. The 'ridge and furrow' design later used in the Crystal Palace may clearly be seen. (The Devonshire Collection, Chatsworth. Reproduced by permission of the Duke of Devonshire and the Chatsworth Settlement Trustees.)

83

which would capture the maximum amount of available sunlight while mitigating the harsher effects of the midday sun. He found that the most favourable results were achieved with a 'ridge and furrow' design in which the roof was covered by a series of narrow, v-shaped 'humps' of the kind illustrated on page 83. He described the results in an article he wrote in the *Magazine of Botany* in 1835:[4]

> 'more morning and evening sun were received, and at an earlier hour, than a flat roof house ... the violence of the mid-day sun was mitigated by the disposition of the angled lights receiving the sun's rays in an oblique direction'.

In the middle was a roadway wide enough for the Duke's carriage

Paxton now incorporated this design, together with other technical innovations, in the construction at Chatsworth of the world's largest conservatory to accommodate the Duke's growing enthusiasm for horticulture. It was begun in 1836 and completed, fully planted, within four years: 277 feet long, 123 feet wide and 67 feet high. In the middle was a roadway wide enough for the Duke's carriage. The first problem was to obtain a supplier of glass. In 1832 Robert Chance had introduced to his Birmingham glassworks some new techniques for making sheet glass that he had discovered in France. Chance offered Paxton sheets of the then unprecedented length of three feet, but Paxton insisted on four feet, reasoning that:[5]

> 'since they had so far advanced as to be able to produce sheets three feet in length, I saw no reason why they should not accomplish another foot; and if this could not be done, I would decline giving the order, as at that time, sheet glass was altogether an experiment in horticultural purposes'.

Presumably this was a bluff, since Paxton needed the glass and it is hard to identify any other source from which he might have obtained it. If it was a bluff then it worked, since Chance agreed to supply the four-foot panels that Paxton wanted. Paxton also designed an innovatory wooden frame to hold the glass panels. Each glazing bar contained three grooves. The glass panel was inserted into the middle groove; the outer groove served as a gutter which trapped rainwater running down the outside of the glass panel and conducted it to downpipes; the inner groove trapped condensation. This design came to be known as 'Paxton's Patent Guttering'. Paxton also designed a machine tool which cut the grooves automatically, powered by a steam engine which he ordered from Boulton and Watt in 1836. Forty miles of glazing bars were prepared in this way. Steam was also used to heat the great conservatory, eight boilers being used to feed seven miles of iron pipework: hence its nickname 'The Great Stove'. In building the conservatory Paxton had made use of three techniques which were later to be employed in the design of the Crystal Palace: large glass panels, a grooved wooden frame and a mechanism for speeding up the process of production and construction. The Great Stove survived for 80 years and was demolished by an engineer called Charles Markham, Joseph Paxton's grandson, shortly after World War One. One further innovation was required before Paxton's Crystal Palace could be conceived and the inspiration for that was provided by another horticultural success.

The Lily House

In 1836 a giant water-lily had been discovered by explorers of the Amazon and in 1846 some of its seeds were received at Kew, where the plant survived but refused to flower. The lily was named *Victoria regia*, later renamed *Victoria amazonica*. In August 1849 Joseph Paxton obtained a specimen of the obstinate plant from his friend Sir William Hooker, the director at Kew. The leaves measured five and a half inches in breadth. Paxton designed a tank to hold the lily in a small conservatory with heating, lighting and humidity reproducing conditions on the Amazon, and a water-wheel gently agitating the water to simulate the conditions of a slowly flowing river. Within a month the leaves had grown from five and a half inches to three and

The Lily House at Chatsworth, built by Paxton to accommodate Victoria Regia. (The Devonshire Collection, Chatsworth. Reproduced by permission of the Duke of Devonshire and the Chatsworth Settlement Trustees.)

a half feet. By November the lily was in full flower and Paxton himself went to Windsor to present Queen Victoria with a bud and leaf. The lily's leaves were now exceeding five feet in diameter and the *Illustrated London News* ran a story under the heading 'The Gigantic Water-Lily at Chatsworth' which reported[6] that Paxton's daughter Annie, aged seven, had stood on one of the leaves in its tank and been comfortably supported. An engraving of Annie in her hazardous position was supplied for the benefit of disbelieving readers. Paxton was impressed by the thin cantilever-like webs that supported the great mass of the leaf. He now had to design, quickly, a new lily house which would accommodate the ever-expanding leaves and the hordes of visitors who came to Chatsworth to see the new phenomenon. The new lily house, accommodating a 33-foot diameter tank, incorporated the 'ridge and furrow' principle adopted for the great conservatory, but its roof was supported by hollow cast-iron pipes which also acted as drainpipes. Joseph Paxton had now made use of all the design principles which would inform the construction of the Crystal Palace.

Paxton's daughter Annie, aged seven, had stood on one of the leaves in its tank and been comfortably supported

The Great Exhibition

Exhibitions of industrial and other artefacts were not unusual in the 19th century. The (later Royal) Society of Arts had staged the first one in 1756, three years after its foundation and from 1847 they became an annual event, that of 1849 being visited by almost 100,000 people.[7] In 1849 Henry Cole (1808–82), soon to become chairman of the Society, visited Paris to see the French national exhibition and upon his return he persuaded Prince Albert, President of the Society, that it would be possible to mount an *international* exhibition in London in 1851, the first of its kind. A special commission was set up to organise the event which included the Prince himself and such eminent figures as Lord John Russell, Sir Robert Peel and William Gladstone. It is now usually forgotten that the proposal attracted a great deal of opposition, especially when the originally proposed site, Somerset House, was abandoned in favour of Hyde Park. The Member of Parliament for Lincoln, Colonel Charles Sibthorp, claimed that moral pollution, revolution and disease (including bubonic plague) would be brought to England by hordes of invading foreigners. His sentiments were supported by *The Times* which complained that:[8]

> *'The whole of Hyde Park and, we will venture to predict, the whole of Kensington Gardens, will be turned into a bivouac of all the vagabonds of London so long as the Exhibition shall continue ... this disreputable spectacle will endure for months'.*

COLONEL CHARLES SIBTHORP (1783–1855)

Charles Sibthorp was born at North Mymms, Hertfordshire, in 1783. He fought under Wellington in the Peninsular War and entered Parliament as MP for Lincoln in 1826. Henceforth he devoted his life to lost causes. Having failed in his opposition to Catholic emancipation in 1829 he opposed the Parliamentary Reform Bill of 1832 and promptly lost his seat to the future Sir Edward Bulwer Lytton, author of *The Last Days of Pompeii*. He re-entered Parliament in 1834 where he was the leader of the 'old order' seeking to preserve the supposed idylls of rural life against the rise of industry and urban living. Sir Robert Peel is reported to have said of him 'There goes a man who is always fearlessly wrong'. He spoke out against Lord Melbourne's proposal to award an allowance of £50,000 a year to Prince Albert and succeeded in having it reduced to £30,000, thereby incurring the lasting enmity of Queen Victoria, who resolved never to visit Lincoln while Sibthorp represented the constituency in Parliament. True to form, Sibthorp supported the Corn Laws as they were being repealed and opposed the passage of the railway through his home town of North Mymms even as it was being built. His views invited caricature and *Punch* often took advantage of this fact. It should be said in his favour that he supported William Wilberforce in his campaign to abolish slavery, though the temporary loss of his seat in 1832 meant that he was unable to vote on the abolition bill of 1833.

At one point the unpopularity of the idea was so great that the Isle of Dogs was suggested as a suitable site. The most pressing problem concerned the design of the building that would house the exhibition. A building committee had been set up which included some of the most eminent architects and engineers of the time. Sir Charles Barry, architect of the Houses of Parliament; the celebrated railway engineers Robert Stephenson and Isambard Kingdom Brunel; and William Cubitt, president of the Institution of Civil Engineers, were all members of the building committee. In March 1850 they invited

Organisers of the Great Exhibition. Prince Albert, seated, examines the plans with a model of the 'Great Stove' at his elbow; Joseph Paxton leans on the table to Albert's right; Charles Barry, seated, faces Albert across the table; the figure standing on the right of the picture is Robert Stephenson. (V & A Picture Library)

designers to submit their proposals within a month and despite this extraordinary deadline, 245 designs were received. Most were hopelessly impractical and submitted by cranks. Twelve of the better ones were submitted by French designers, including the designer of the market at Les Halles in Paris. Eighteen were singled out for 'higher honorary distinction'. The flattering title could not, however, conceal the fact that none of the designs satisfied the committee, which then produced its own proposal, mostly the work of Brunel. Brunel's record as a designer of railways, bridges, ships and railway stations is second to none, but his proposed design for the Great Exhibition, no doubt conceived in haste and possibly influenced by his fellow committee members, was not a happy one in either practical or aesthetic terms. It would have required 15 million bricks and it was by no means certain that such a quantity could be produced in the time available. One writer has described it as:[9]

> 'a vast, squat, brick warehouse four times the length and twice the width of St Paul's Cathedral. This was to be adorned with a monstrous iron dome which, even though it was bigger than that of the cathedral, would have looked like no more than a bowler hat on a billiard table'.

SIR HENRY COLE (1808–82)

Henry Cole was the son of an army recruiting officer and attended Christ's Hospital School. At the age of 15 he obtained a job as a clerk at the Record Commission, the forerunner of the Public Record Office, where he orchestrated a campaign against the waste and corruption that prevailed in that neglected branch of the civil service. It was at this time that he learned to use publicity and journalism in support of ideas that he favoured. In 1838 he met Rowland Hill and helped him to introduce the Penny Post, Cole himself being responsible for engaging artists to design the stamps. In 1850 he became chairman of the Society for the Encouragement of Arts, Manufacturers and Commerce, later the Royal Society of Arts, and it was in this capacity that he became involved in planning the Great Exhibition of 1851. It was Cole who suggested to Prince Albert that the exhibition should be international, the first such exhibition ever mounted. He was instrumental in using the profits of the Great Exhibition to begin the process of creating the South Kensington museums district and was the first director of the Victoria and Albert Museum. He later raised money for the construction of the Albert Hall. He was knighted in 1875. His vigorous campaigning style made him, in the words of the Prime Minister Lord Derby 'The most generally unpopular man I know' and he incurred the wrath of Ruskin[10] for advocating the application of art to the products of industry. In that respect, as in others, he was ahead of his time.

Contemporary enthusiasm for Brunel's design was no greater than that of this later critic, so it is not surprising that it was at this time that Prince Albert contemplated abandoning the whole idea, being persuaded to continue only by the redoubtable Henry Cole.

A piece of blotting paper

It was at this point that Joseph Paxton chanced to visit John Ellis MP, chairman of the Midland Railway, at the House of Commons. Paxton had been a director of the Midland Railway since 1848 and the purpose of his visit to the House, on 7 June 1850, was to offer an opinion on the acoustics of the building, which was nearing completion after the disastrous fire of 1834. Paxton suggested that the acoustic problems that the building was beginning to display might be overshadowed by a much greater fiasco in the design of the Exhibition building. Ellis agreed and suggested that any ideas which Paxton could produce, even at this late stage, would no doubt be welcomed by the building committee. Ellis took Paxton by cab to see Henry Cole, who assured him that, if he could produce a suitable design, he would find a way around the fact that the competition for the building was technically closed.

a much greater fiasco in the design of the Exhibition building

Four days later, on 11 June, Paxton visited Derby, the headquarters of the Midland Railway, to chair a committee of the railway. One of the items on the agenda concerned the supposed failure of a pointsman to attend properly to his duties. During the discussion of this and other similarly interesting matters the chairman was observed by other members of the committee to be doodling on a piece of blotting paper. The blotting paper, which is now preserved in the Victoria and Albert Museum, contained a proposed design for the exhibition building, based upon the lily house at Chatsworth, though on an heroic scale. Having imposed a fine of five shillings on the errant pointsman Paxton proceeded to Chatsworth, where he enlisted the help of his staff to produce a set of working drawings for the structure. He also secured the assistance of William Henry Barlow (1812–1902), resident engineer of the Midland Railway, who calculated the required strength of the columns and girders that would support the building. Barlow was the brother of Peter Barlow, who had built the Tower subway and developed Marc Brunel's tunnelling shield for the construction of the City and South London Railway.[11]

Paxton's blotting paper. (V & A Picture Library)

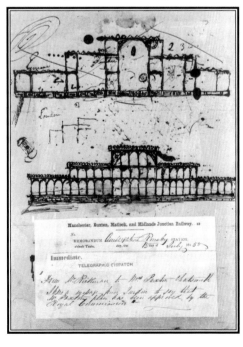

The designs had been completed in the incredible time of eight days when Paxton, on 20 June, returned by train to London to present them to the Exhibition building committee. As he waited for the train at Derby he encountered Robert Stephenson, a member of the committee, who was by chance making his way to London. Paxton shared a compartment with the great railway engineer and asked for his opinion of the design. Stephenson lit a cigar and began to examine the plans with care. His attention was so fully engaged by the plans he was examining, that he failed to notice that the cigar had gone out. Finally he rolled up the plans, uttered the single word 'admirable' and promised Paxton that he would ensure they were seen by the committee.

Stephenson rolled up the plans, uttered the single word 'admirable'

ROBERT STEPHENSON (1803–59)

Robert, the only son of George Stephenson, was born in Northumberland and in 1822 helped his father to survey the line of the Stockton and Darlington Railway, which opened in September 1825, the world's first. In 1823 the father and son founded the world's first locomotive manufacturing company in Newcastle, from which locomotives were exported throughout the world, many going to the US and Germany. In 1824 Robert went to South America for three years to work in gold and silver mines. On his return he worked with his father on the design of the *Rocket,* which won the Rainhill trials of 1829 and set the pattern for the future development of steam locomotives. In 1833 he became chief engineer of the London to Birmingham Railway with its terminus at Euston and he designed the Britannia tubular bridge at the Menai Straits in North Wales as well as bridges across the Nile and at Montreal. In 1847 he became MP for Whitby and thereafter served on many committees concerned with engineering works. When he died in 1859 his remains were interred in Westminster Abbey.

Leaving nothing to chance, Paxton decided to reveal his plans to the *Illustrated London News*, which had shown great interest in his previous designs such as the lily house. The account of the building, in extremely flattering terms, no doubt owed much to Paxton's own descriptive gifts.[12] It told of:

'a building for the exhibition of arts and manufactures that, while it afforded ample accommodation for the purposes intended would, of itself, be the most singular

*and peculiar feature of the Exhibition ... Mr Paxton
ventures to think that such a plan would meet with the
almost universal approval of the British public, whilst it
would be unrivalled in the world'.*

This verdict was not far from that of the paper's readers and of the
building committee itself, who asked Paxton to find a firm of
contractors which would submit a tender to agree to construct and
erect the design, the tender to be submitted by 10 July. Paxton now
contacted Robert Chance, supplier of glass for the Great Stove, and
Charles Fox of the engineering firm Fox and Henderson.[13] Charles Fox
was by background a railway engineer, having designed the
locomotive *Novelty* which had competed with the Stephensons'
Rocket in the Rainhill trials of 1829. Fox agreed to prepare a detailed
set of engineers' drawings and a tender for the building and further
frantic work now ensued to meet the apparently impossible deadline,
with Fox himself regularly working 18-hour days for seven weeks.
Paxton made frequent visits to Fox's offices at Smethwick and Spring
Gardens, Westminster.[14] On one occasion he was joined by Henry
Cole, on behalf of the Commissioners of the Exhibition, who was
anxious to ensure that the design was not rejected on some technical
ground: as clear an indication as anyone could wish of the
Commissioners' enthusiasm for the design. At a late stage a transept
was incorporated into the design of the building with a circular roof
like that on the Great Stove, so as to accommodate some of Hyde
Park's large elm trees within the structure of the building itself. Brunel,
whose own design was threatened by Paxton's, provided his rival with
details of the heights of the trees to be accommodated, explaining that
'I mean to win with our [i.e. the committee's] plan but I have thought
it right to give your beautiful plan all the advantages that it is
susceptible of'. Was this an example of Brunel's magnanimity, or had
he, like the rest of the committee, realised that Paxton's plan was
really the only one that mattered?

The tender was submitted by the required date incorporating the
principles already employed by Paxton in his novel structures at
Chatsworth: extensive use of plate glass; cast iron supporting columns
which also acted as drainpipes; a wooden frame for the roof with
mechanically produced triple grooves for trapping condensation and
rainwater as well as holding the glass; and a 'ridge and furrow' roof
design to make best use of the sunlight. One further innovation was a
four-wheeled 'glazing wagon'. This was designed to run in the outer
gutters of 'Paxton's Patent Guttering' and enabled two men and a boy
to work at once, inserting the sheets of glass as the wagon moved

*Fox himself
regularly working
18-hour days for
seven weeks*

along the roof of the building. Fox Henderson tendered to construct the building for £150,000 or for the lower price of £78,900 if, when dismantled, it reverted to the ownership of Fox Henderson for re-erection elsewhere. The Commissioners, greatly relieved, accepted the tender. The Crystal Palace, as *Punch* dubbed Paxton's design, would house the Great Exhibition.

Dire warnings

The opposition to the Exhibition, and the Crystal Palace, now rallied for the last time. The ever-hopeful Colonel Sibthorp warned that the summer heat inside the glass edifice would be intolerable and would be responsible for sickness or even deaths. He was unaware of the palliative effects on the sun's rays of Paxton's 'ridge and furrow' roof and of the fact that Paxton had taken the precaution of specifying that the roof should be covered with white canvas as an additional protection. The Astronomer Royal, Sir George Airy, added his voice to those of the critics when he declared that a wind of 'moderate force' would bring down the building. As construction proceeded amid winds of more than moderate force this argument withdrew to be replaced by others. Hail, it was claimed, would shatter the glass, but the hail that fell failed to live up to the expectations of the doomsayers. Finally it was prophesied that the proposed opening ceremony would be a catastrophe. Either the 21-gun salute in Hyde Park, to mark the arrival of the Queen and Prince Consort, would cause the glass to shatter; or if that failed then the musical accompaniment of 600 voices, 200 instruments and the palace's organ would do the trick. Even as construction proceeded the Institution of Civil Engineers devoted an evening to a discussion of the building's shortcomings and the likely catastrophic consequences of its use, though it may be suggested that the members were alarmed that a mere gardener, like Paxton, could design on a piece of blotting paper

the 21-gun salute in Hyde Park would cause the glass to shatter

a building that had defeated the Institution's finest. Paxton, Fox and the Commissioners ignored these dire warnings and began the work of construction which now proceeded apace. They were no doubt reassured by the confidence of their former rival, Brunel, who declared that the design was 'the best adapted in every respect for the purpose for which it was intended'.[15]

Building the Crystal Palace

The building had been designed to make the maximum use of standardised components, the standard measure being 24 feet. Thus it was 1,848 feet long by 408 feet wide with an extension 936 feet by 48 feet on part of the north side. The components were manufactured off-site and assembled on the south side of Hyde Park. The main entrance was on the south side of the building near Prince of Wales Gate and extended over the area to the south of Rotten Row. An upper tier of galleries gave a total floor space of almost a million square feet, with one and three quarter miles of galleries. The roof alone comprised almost 18 acres and the enclosed space was six times that of St Paul's Cathedral.

The building was erected in the astonishing time of 22 weeks and painted and fitted out in a further 16. Work began in September 1850. First the foundations were installed, these consisting of cast-iron base plates, which looked like upturned mushrooms with hollow stems, into which the supporting cast-iron down-pipes were inserted. As each section of the metal structure was completed 'Paxton's patent guttering' was installed, with its three grooves for condensation, glass and rainwater. It was at this point that Paxton's glazing wagons came into use. Seventy-six were used, each carrying its three-man crew. The wagons ran along the outer grooves as the crew installed the sheets of glass – more than a million square feet in all – supplied by Robert Chance, who had recruited skilled glass-blowers in France to enable

'the best adapted in every respect for the purpose for which it was intended'

The Crystal Palace. (By courtesy of the Guildhall Library, Corporation of London)

Paxton's patent glazing wagon.

him to meet the demand. An opening in the centre of each wagon allowed additional supplies of glass, bars and putty to be hauled up from below. Curved iron stays, like those on a covered wagon, permitted a canvas roof to be deployed so that work could continue during inclement weather. By this means 18,000 panes could be installed in a single week regardless of the weather.

The construction site became a spectacle in its own right. By December 1850, with the work at its height, the workforce had reached 2,260 and the contractors were able to charge five shillings to the many visitors who wanted to enter the site to see the work in progress. Presumably some of them were hoping to see it fall down in accordance with the confident predictions of the Astronomer Royal, but as the months passed they were disappointed. There were some unforeseen problems that were dealt with by the Duke of Wellington. One of the many offices held by the 82-year-old soldier was that of Park Ranger of Hyde Park, so to him fell the task of evicting a squatter called Mrs Hicks who had taken up residence in a wooden cabin close to the site, from which she sold cakes and water. On November 15 he wrote that 'We have got rid of the Squatter in the Park. She has quitted her Residence, which has been pulled down and the ground on which it stood or rather fell has been levelled'[16] The Queen herself consulted the Duke about another delicate problem when birds began to nest in the elms contained within the building. The prospect of royalty, among others, being bombarded from above with bird droppings would not, it was felt, add to the dignity of the Exhibition. The Duke recommended the use of sparrowhawks and no more was heard of the matter.

'We have got rid of the Squatter in the Park'

The building, when completed in time for the scheduled opening date of the Great Exhibition, met with almost universal praise. Brunel's generous verdict has already been noted but praise also came from sources which appreciated the building more than the engineering skill with which it had been designed and built. The Exhibition opened on 1 May 1851, and Thackeray celebrated it with a May-Day Ode:

> But yesterday a naked sod
> The dandies sneered from Rotten Row,
> And cantered o'er it to and fro:
>   And see 'tis done!
> As though 'twere by a wizard's rod
> A blazing arch of lucid glass
> Leaps like a fountain from the grass
>   To meet the sun!

Punch took a different line. Drawing attention to the endless delays that had attended the rebuilding of the Houses of Parliament it suggested that the job should be handed to Paxton: 'Mr Paxton you *must* achieve the Glass Houses of Parliament'. There were a few disapproving voices, notably that of the influential art critic John Ruskin, who dismissed the building as 'a greenhouse larger than ever greenhouse was built before' and complained that glass lacked 'form'[17] This was a curious judgement, as well as a minority one, from an admirer of mediaeval architecture who had presumably overlooked the huge expanses of glass used by the mediaeval builders of the great East Anglian churches like Southwold.

'a greenhouse larger than ever greenhouse was built before'

The Exhibition opens

The opening ceremony, on 1 May, was as grand an occasion as may be imagined. The Archbishop of Canterbury said a short prayer and the Hallelujah Chorus was performed by the mass choir and orchestra. Neither this nor the 21-gun salute from Hyde Park brought the edifice crashing down, as some had confidently predicted, but during the singing a mysterious Chinaman, in Mandarin dress, who was not present in any official capacity, stepped forward and executed a low bow to the Queen. The Lord Chamberlain was then commanded by the Queen to declare the Exhibition open.[18] The Queen recorded her own feelings in her journal for that day: 'This day is one of the greatest and most glorious days of our lives, with which to my pride and joy the name of my dearly beloved Albert is for ever associated'.

The Queen's enthusiasm was shared by her subjects. During the

The Great Exhibition opening ceremony. Paxton is the figure on the left of the picture in knee breeches and white hose and next to him is Charles Fox, whose firm built the palace. Just in front of Fox is Henry Cole. The mysterious Chinaman may be seen on the right. (V & A Picture Library)

it was visited by 6,039,195 people, almost the same number as visited the Millennium Dome 150 years later

five and a half months before the Great Exhibition closed on 15 October 1851 (a closure caused by the fading autumn light and the inadequacy of the gas lights in the building itself), it was visited by 6,039,195 people, almost the same number as visited the Millennium Dome 150 years later from a vastly greater population with better transport facilities. Nevertheless, the huge number of visitors was made possible by the enterprise of the fledgling railway companies like Brunel's Great Western, Paxton's Midland and Robert Stephenson's London and Birmingham Railway. Excursion trains were organised to enable travellers from the provinces to visit

View of the British Department of the Great Exhibition of 1851. (By courtesy of the Guildhall Library, Corporation of London)

London, often for the first time, and to experience the eighth wonder of the world. The number of visitors was also increased by the intelligence of the Commissioners in pricing their admission tickets. Since the Exhibition was closed on Sundays it was open to visitors for 141 days altogether. In all 13,494 season tickets for men were sold at a price of three guineas each, with 12,111 being sold for women at the unaccountably lower price of two guineas.[19] For the first two days visitors were charged the substantial sum of one pound to enter the exhibition, but thereafter the prices were gradually reduced to five shillings (about a day's wages for a skilled workman); then to half a crown and, for the last 80 days, to one shilling, this last figure accounting for 4,439,419 visitors, or almost three quarters of the total.

The astonished visitors saw 112,000 separate exhibits from 7,381 British and 6,556 foreign exhibitors. They were broadly divided into five categories: Raw Materials (ranging from coal to peacock feathers); Machinery (mostly concerned with industrial machines with Britain, Germany and the upcoming United States well represented, the last particularly so in agricultural machinery); Manufactures (from Swiss watches to a pair of cuffs made from poodle fur); Fine Arts (featuring a statue of the Prince of Wales improbably presented as a Greek shepherd); and a Miscellaneous category. The Miscellaneous category defies summary beyond saying that its contents were mostly bizarre, including a life-size human figure which could be expanded to twice its size by manipulating thousands of concealed moving parts. Cities like Birmingham and Sheffield had their own exhibits, as did colonies like India, Canada and the West Indies, as well as foreign nations like Austria, Persia, Greece and France. France won more medals than any other nation.

One of the most successful items on show was not an exhibit at all but an amenity. The water-closet had grown in popularity during the early part of the 19th century owing to design improvements made in the previous century. An enterprising manufacturer of the newly-fashionable devices called George Jennings installed some of his own models in the Exhibition building and charged visitors a penny to use them. 827,000 visitors took advantage of this opportunity, many of them no doubt 'spending a penny' for the first time and thereby adding a new phrase to the language. George Jennings's devices had helped the visitors to dispose of the 1,092,332 bottles of soft drinks and 1,813,718 buns that were consumed at the Exhibition and his business subsequently prospered. *Punch* lamented the fact that 'Nothing stronger than

'spending a penny' for the first time and thereby adding a new phrase to the language

The refreshments were supplied by an ambitious little company called Schweppes

ginger-beer is to be sold in the way of refreshment', commenting that this would make a strange impression on foreign visitors. The refreshments were supplied by an ambitious little company called Schweppes.

The Exhibition attracted many distinguished visitors in addition to the millions of shilling ticket holders. The Queen herself visited the Exhibition on more than 40 occasions and the Duke of Wellington, who died a few months after the Exhibition closed, was also a frequent visitor. On one occasion his presence caused a commotion. This was on 7 October 1851, a week before the Exhibition closed, when a record number of 109,915 people were admitted. As the crowds among whom he was moving recognised him they began to cheer, causing others further distant to mistake the cheering for cries of alarm. Some thought that the building was collapsing. A stampede by some to leave the building ensued but the only casualty was a stand containing French porcelain which was overturned. There were no other accidents – a fine record to which should be added the note that no fatalities occurred during the construction of the building itself.

When the Exhibition closed its doors the Commissioners were able to make some very satisfying calculations. The accounts of the Exhibition read as follows:[20]

Receipts	£522,179
Expenses	£335,742
Surplus	**£186,437**

Paxton and Fox were knighted for their services and Paxton received a bounty of £5,000. The surplus was later used to buy the land which was used for the South Kensington museums sites, including Alfred Waterhouse's Natural History Museum,[21] and Henry Cole was knighted for his role in creating these in 1875.

What to do with the Crystal Palace

There now arose the question of what to do with the building itself, which had always been intended as a temporary resident of Hyde Park. Paxton himself, not surprisingly, suggested that it might remain in place as a 'Winter Garden' and he was supported in this by Henry Cole, who wrote a pamphlet under the name 'Denarius' which bore the suggestive title 'Shall we keep the Crystal Palace and have Riding and Walking in all Weathers among Flowers, Fountains and Sculpture?' To this the answer was a resounding 'no' from both Prince Albert and, more importantly, the House of Commons, which voted, on 29 April 1852, to dismantle it. Sir Titus Salt made enquiries about removing it to his industrial complex at Saltaire in Yorkshire but this and other projects were overtaken by events when, within three weeks of the Commons vote, the Crystal Palace Company issued a prospectus which called for investors to subscribe £500,000 with a view to re-erecting the building on a site at Sydenham, south London. Given the success of the Great Exhibition it is not surprising that the shares were greatly over-subscribed.

The new enterprise was different in character from the Exhibition, as was the building itself. It is significant that the chairman of the company, of which Paxton was himself a director, was Samuel Laing, also chairman of the London, Brighton and South Coast Railway. The original prospectus specified that there would be a railway station within the building itself. The promoters eventually had to be contented with a station within the grounds but it is clear that Laing had seen the amount of extra traffic generated for the railways by the Exhibition and wanted to make this a permanent feature of his own line's prosperity. His ambitions were those shown by Sir Edward Watkin of the Metropolitan Railway when Watkin proposed the 'Neasden Tower' 40 years later.[22] The company prospectus promised:

> *'Refined recreation, calculated to elevate the intellect, to instruct the mind, to improve the heart, will welcome the millions who now have no other incentive to pleasure but such as the gin palace, the dancing saloon and the ale-house afford them'.*

The company never quite achieved these lofty aims.

The New Crystal Palace

The promoters first had to move the building to Sydenham. Since there was as yet no local rail service, the huge quantities of materials had to be moved mostly by horse and cart 20 miles to the new site, the last stretch being up a steep incline to the hilltop eminence that the company had purchased. The building was also redesigned so that it was almost one-and-a-half times the size of the original, with three transepts instead of one. Brunel, an admirer of the original building and a keen supporter of the Sydenham venture, designed two huge water towers for the new site which were required to supply the 11,788 water jets and fountains that Paxton proposed to install in the surrounding gardens. It is hard to avoid the conclusion that all concerned had been carried away by the success of the Great

reported that a tavern called 'The Sibthorpe's Head' was to be opened in the grounds of the new palace

View of the Crystal Palace and park at Sydenham, showing the terraces, water towers, fountains, lakes, dinosaurs and other additions to the original structure. (By courtesy of the Guildhall Library, Corporation of London)

'It's superb! What a place for a fete!'

Exhibition which had occupied a site in central London for a short period. The prospects of reproducing that success over a long period at a site far from conveniently situated were tempting but unrealistic. It took almost two years to erect the building (compared with nine months for the original), 12 fatalities were incurred during the construction work and the cost was almost £1,300,000. *Punch*, in an ironic reference to the doughtiest opponent of the original Crystal Palace, reported that a tavern called 'The Sibthorpe's Head' was to be opened in the grounds of the new palace.[23]

The new palace opened on 10 June 1854, to the customary Hallelujah Chorus, and offered attractions similar to those of the Exhibition itself, including manufactured goods, geological specimens and statues.[24] To these were added historical tableaux of the kind later associated with Madame Tussaud's. In the grounds Professor Richard Owen, keeper of Natural History collections at the British Museum, mounted a display of cement dinosaurs (a word Owen himself coined). At this time there was little competition from museums in central London. The British Museum was designed for scholarship rather than entertainment and the Natural History Museum, built as a consequence of Owen's urgent promptings, would not become a serious competitor for another quarter of a century.[25] Firework displays and brass band concerts became regular features of the entertainment provided and the new site attracted its share of distinguished visitors. Both the Queen and the French Emperor Napoleon III visited, the latter commenting 'It's superb! What a place for a fete!'[26]

Despite such testimonies the new Crystal Palace never prospered as the old one had. In December 1866 a fire destroyed one of the extra transepts that Paxton had incorporated in the Sydenham building and it was not rebuilt. In 1909 the company, on the verge of bankruptcy, appointed a receiver who brought about some modest revival in its fortunes by introducing the world's first motor museum. During World War One it served as a naval barracks and when the war ended it provided a first, temporary home for the Imperial War Museum, trading at a modest profit. Its final moment came on 30 November 1936, with a fire which began in some administrative offices and spread quickly, fed by the more than 20 miles of wooden 'Paxton's patent guttering' in the roof. The blaze was visible from the South Downs.

Paxton's later works

Sir Joseph Paxton had not finished with glass, or with London, when he moved to Rockhills, a house on the Sydenham site in 1853. He was invited to design a Crystal Palace for New York, which was never built, and a country home for the Rothschilds at Mentmore, Buckinghamshire, which became the home of the Earl of Rosebery, who was briefly Prime Minister in succession to Gladstone. Mentmore is noted for its imaginative use of glass in its huge windows, which give a feeling of light and spaciousness to the building.

In 1855 Sir Joseph Paxton appeared before a Parliamentary Committee with a proposal to overcome London's chronic transport problems.[27] His proposal was for a 'Grand Girdle Railway and Boulevard under Glass' to be patriotically named 'The Great Victorian Way'. This was a railway, 12 miles long, built above ground but within a glass arcade to protect travellers from the London air fouled by the stench of smoke from chimneys and from the sewage which floated in the Thames. Within the glass arcade would be shops and houses. The railway would link all London's main line railway termini, would cross the river three times on enclosed bridges and would carry passengers during the day and freight at night. He suggested that, for those fortunate enough to occupy houses within the glass arcade, it would be 'almost equal to going to a foreign climate and would prevent many infirm persons being obliged to go into foreign countries in the winter'. The Parliamentarians commended Sir Joseph for a proposal which 'possesses many features of remarkable novelty' but baulked at the cost of £34 million. By comparison, Brunel's Great Western Railway cost £6 million and Sir Joseph Bazalgette's main drainage £4 million.

Five years later Paxton made a more useful contribution to London's future when he proposed the establishment of a Select

a glass arcade to protect travellers from the London air

Committee on the embankment of the Thames.[28] Paxton chaired the committee which supported Joseph Bazalgette's proposal to embank the Thames between Westminster Bridge and Blackfriars Bridge to provide a new roadway as well as a route for the new underground railway and, most importantly, Bazalgette's main intercepting sewer. This great engineering work, which thus owed something to Paxton's support, is described in Chapter 6.

Sir Joseph Paxton died on 8 June 1865 at Rockhills, Sydenham. The many obituary tributes included references to his noble character as well as his achievements. *The Builder* attributed much of his success to his 'readiness to accord credit to others' while *The Times* declared that 'He rose from the ranks to be the greatest gardener of his time, the founder of a new style of architecture, and a man of genius, who devoted it to objects in the highest and noblest sense popular'. Perhaps Robert Stephenson had already said the most important thing about Joseph Paxton. Born in the same year as Paxton, first to see the drawings for the Crystal Palace on that train journey from Derby to London, he told *The Times* in the year of the Great Exhibition 'without Paxton we should never have had a Crystal Palace'. And without the Crystal Palace there might have been no Great Exhibition, no profit and no museums in South Kensington.

Paxton's 'Great Victorian Way'; an impossibly expensive solution to Victorian London's transport problems. (London's Transport Museum)

[1] The account of Paxton's early life is based upon material in *Joseph Paxton*, by John Anthony, Shire Publications, 1973.

[2] See page 25 for an account of the work of Decimus Burton.

[3] See Chapter 1 for an account of this strange relationship.

[4] *Magazine of Botany*, 1835, volume 11, page 80.

[5] *Transactions of the Royal Society of Arts*, volume 57, 1850; Paxton's lecture.

[6] *Illustrated London News*, 17 November 1849, page 328.

[7] *King Cole* by Elizabeth Bonython, Victoria & Albert Museum, 1982, gives a good account of these earlier events and of the career of Sir Henry Cole (1808–82).

[8] *The Times*, 25 June 1850.

[9] *Paxton's Palace*, by Anthony Bird, Cassell, 1976, page 22.

[10] See page 174 for an account of the work of John Ruskin.

[11] See page 46 for this reference.

[12] *Illustrated London News*, 6 July 1850, volume 17, page 13.

[13] Later and better known as Freeman Fox and Partners.

[14] Later the offices of Sir Joseph Bazalgette, whose contributions to London's infrastructure are described in Chapter 6.

[15] *Victorian Engineering*, L.T.C. Rolt, Penguin, 1988, page 151.

[16] Correspondence with Lady Salisbury; *Paxton's Palace*, Anthony Bird, Cassell, 1976, page 76.

[17] *The Stones of Venice*, John Ruskin, volume 1, appendix 17.

[18] *King Cole* by Elizabeth Bonython, Victoria & Albert Museum, 1982, page 37.
[19] *Paxton's Palace*, by Anthony Bird, Cassell, 1976, page 112 et seq. contains many of the details that follow.
[20] *Paxton's Palace*, by Anthony Bird, Cassell, 1976, page 118.
[21] See Chapter 8 for an account of Waterhouse's work.
[22] See Chapter 7 for an account of this episode.
[23] *Punch*, 1852, volume 22, page 237.
[24] *The Works of Sir Joseph Paxton*, George F. Chadwick, Architectural Press, 1961, Chapter 6.
[25] See Chapter 8 for an account of the construction of the Natural History Museum.
[26] *The Works of Sir Joseph Paxton*, George F. Chadwick, Architectural Press, 1961, page 155 note 34.
[27] Parliamentary papers, 1854–5, volume 10, pages 78 et seq.
[28] *Hansard*, volume 158, 4 May 1860, column 736.

CHAPTER 5

Sir Charles Barry and the New Palace of Westminster

'He would rather be a Commissioner than the successful competitor, to be hunted and pursued with every species of invective in the way that Mr Barry had been'.
(Sir Robert Peel, speaking in the House of Commons, 1836, about Sir Charles Barry's design for the New Palace of Westminster)

'Sir Christopher Wren had to deal with men who knew what they wanted ... I am sorry to say that august assembly which has most to do with the erection of this magnificent structure has in it a vast number of men who ask questions, make suggestions and offer criticisms, while at the same time they do not know what is wanted or, indeed, what they want themselves'.
(Lord de Grey, sympathising with Barry for the ill-informed criticism levelled against him)

Sir Charles Barry (1795–1860). (By courtesy of the National Portrait Gallery, London)

SIR CHARLES Barry (1795–1860) was the architect responsible for designing the New Palace of Westminster after the mediaeval building was mostly destroyed in the fire of 1834. His son, Sir John Wolfe-Barry (1836–1918) was the engineer who, with Sir Horace Jones, designed and built Tower

The old Palace of Westminster. (By courtesy of the Guildhall Library, Corporation of London)

Bridge. Between them the father and son created two of London's most celebrated landmarks. Yet there must have been times when the father regretted winning the contract that was to bring him lasting fame.

Born in the shadow of the palace

Charles Barry was born on 13 May 1795, in Bridge Street, Westminster, close to the Palace of Westminster and in a house which, 60 years later, was literally in the shadow of the clock tower which would be the most prominent feature of Barry's design for the new palace. He attended Christ's Hospital School, which was at that time located on the north side of Newgate, just south of the present site of St Bartholomew's Hospital in the City of London. In 1811 he was articled to a firm of surveyors in Lambeth. His son, Dr Alfred Barry (1826–1910), later principal of King's College London and archbishop of Sydney, recorded in his biography of his father[1] that in his childhood Charles, the only member of his family to show any artistic tendencies, had been in the habit of drawing on the walls of his bedroom in Bridge Street. The wallpaper was replaced when it no longer had any space for further designs. This helps to explain how it was that, during his period of apprenticeship, the young Charles Barry regularly exhibited at the Royal Academy. His first exhibit, with unconscious foresight in view of his later work, was entitled 'A view of the interior of Westminster Hall'. Westminster Hall was one of the few buildings to survive the conflagration of 1834 which destroyed both Houses of Parliament, and Barry designed his new palace around the surviving structure of Richard II's famous mediaeval hall. Barry was elected a Royal Academician in 1844.

Barry's father, a prosperous stationer, had died in 1805, leaving a considerable sum to be inherited by his son when he reached the age of 21, so in 1817, fortified by his inheritance, Charles quit his articles and set about broadening his education. The continent had reopened to English travellers following the end of the Napoleonic Wars in 1815, so Barry embarked on a European tour following a route very similar to that travelled by Alfred Waterhouse 38 years later. He visited Italy, Greece and Constantinople, where, like Waterhouse,[2] he particularly admired Justinian's Aya Sophia, a building almost unknown in Western Europe at that time. The tour was not without incident. On one occasion in Italy Barry was sketching some buildings of interest when he was approached by a group of soldiers who asked to see his passport. Barry dismissed them but they followed him back to his lodgings and attempted to arrest him, leaving only when Barry shouted at them and produced a gun to add emphasis to his exclamations.[3] While in Rome Barry, now running short of money, met a wealthy Englishman called David Baillie who offered to buy Barry's considerable collection of sketches for £200 and invited the young artist to accompany him to Egypt and the Holy Land. Barry copied his sketches before handing over the originals to his benefactor and then spent a further period with Baillie cruising up the Nile and visiting the Holy Land while adding to his, and Baillie's, collection of architectural sketches. During their visit to what is now Syria they were temporarily abducted by their Arab guides who were convinced that their English visitors must be in search of buried treasure. They were released when their captors finally became convinced that they really were interested only in the curious pastime of visiting and sketching ruined buildings. During his return to England Barry met a man called John Wolfe whom he had known during the time that they were both serving apprenticeships in Lambeth. Wolfe was to remain a lifelong friend.

Early works
Upon his return to England, in 1820, Barry married and established himself in practice in Ely Place, Holborn. There followed a series of commissions[4] which began with requests from various ecclesiastical sources for churches to be built at modest costs. One evangelical clergyman even devised a plan to build 'churches for nothing'[5] which cannot have been either attractive or profitable to a struggling

Barry shouted at them and produced a gun to add emphasis to his exclamations

One evangelical clergyman even devised a plan to build 'churches for nothing'

architect whose fee was normally 5 percent of the construction costs. He also made a number of unsuccessful entries to design competitions, notably for Westminster Hospital and Birmingham town hall. He was, however, successful in gaining the contract for the design of King Edward VI's School, Birmingham, which brought him into contact with two fellow professionals, Augustus Pugin and John Thomas, who were later to work with him on the Palace of Westminster. At one point Barry considered emigrating to America in search of more remunerative work but eventually his patience and diligence were rewarded in London. Through a contact made in Rome Barry had secured an introduction to Lord and Lady Holland of the powerful Whig 'Holland House Set' and it may have been through contacts made there that in 1829 he secured the contract for his first major public building: the Travellers' Club, Pall Mall. In 1837 this was followed by the design for the nearby Reform Club. Some commentators have detected in the latter building echoes of the Palazzo Farnese in Florence, which Barry had sketched on his tour 10 years earlier.

The Palace of Westminster, including both Houses of Parliament, was ablaze

The conflagration

On 16 October 1834, as he returned in his carriage from an appointment in south London, Charles Barry noticed a glow in the sky from the vicinity of Westminster. The Palace of Westminster, including both Houses of Parliament, was ablaze. The inferno had been caused by an early, if misguided, attempt at recycling. Since the Middle Ages the Court of Exchequer had issued receipts for taxes paid in the form

View along Pall Mall with the Reform Club to the right. (By courtesy of the Guildhall Library, Corporation of London)

of wooden tallies. These were split down the middle, one half being kept by the taxpayer and the other stored by the court in the Palace of Westminster. The practice had continued until 1826, by which time every inch of storage space in the palace was occupied by these decaying relics of mediaeval taxation. An enterprising official suggested that they be used as fuel for the building's antiquated heating system. The rotting timber burned so merrily that the blaze soon extended from the boiler to the remainder of the building. The Prime Minister, Lord Melbourne, and the Chancellor of the Exchequer, Lord Althorp, hurried to the scene. They saw the House of Lords Chamber ablaze and the flames advancing on St Stephen's Chapel, which since 1530 had served as the meeting place for the House of Commons. Beyond the chapel lay Richard II's Westminster Hall, scene of some of the most memorable events in English history, including the trials of Thomas More, Guy Fawkes and Charles I. Althorp spoke for both of them when he cried 'Damn the House of Commons. Let it blaze but save the Hall'. Westminster Hall survived together with the crypt and a few fragments of St Stephen's Chapel. With these exceptions the building was destroyed. The 'Mother of Parliaments' was homeless.

'Damn the House of Commons. Let it blaze but save the Hall'

King William IV's Government, headed by Lord Melbourne, considered rebuilding the palace on a different site. The Thames-side location, on Thorney Island, was far from ideal before the embankment of the river and by 1834 the Thames was receiving a steadily increasing proportion of London's sewage, a fact that would precipitate the crisis of 'The Great Stink' 24 years later.[5] Both Green Park and Trafalgar Square were considered as alternative sites but dismissed as impractical. On 3 June 1835, a Select Committee set out the specifications for the new palace, which included the requirements 'that the style of the building be either Gothic or Elizabethan'; that the House of Commons should have seating for 460 members; and that the palace should contain two prison cells to accommodate persons who behaved disrespectfully towards Parliament.[7] Plans were to be submitted by 1 November 1835 and 'premiums' (payments) of £500 each were promised for the entries selected by the Commissioners whom the King appointed to judge them. A striking feature of the competition, at a time when public expenditure was regarded as little less than a vice, was the decision of the Commissioners that 'we are not called upon to make the cost of any design an object of our consideration'.[8]

the palace should contain two prison cells to accommodate persons who behaved disrespectfully towards Parliament

The design chosen was that of Charles Barry, who had laboured for up to 20 hours a day for over three months to submit his designs on time. He had also visited cities in the Low Countries to study Gothic monumental buildings[9,] as Waterhouse was to do when preparing his own designs 30 years later.[10] He had built his design around the surviving Westminster Hall and also incorporated the crypt of St Stephen's Chapel, thereby preserving in the new Gothic building the best surviving features of the mediaeval one. In January 1836 the commissioners declared that:

> 'we are all unanimous in our opinion that the design delivered to us, with the emblem of a portcullis, bears throughout such evident marks of genius as fully to entitle it to the preference we have given it'.[11]

It was calculated that the buildings would cost £693,104 and a further £129,000 would be needed to purchase land and embank the Thames. The unanimity of the commissioners was not reflected in the opinions of Barry's fellow-architects, 96 of whom had made unsuccessful entries to the competition. On 22 June 1836, a group of them presented a petition to the House of Commons requesting that the competition be reopened. There followed a prolonged wrangle over the suitability of the design, which was the subject of an ill-tempered debate in the House of Commons.[12] One MP described Barry's design as 'a fine picture, well calculated to deceive one young and inexperienced in architecture' while another claimed that 'the data on which Mr Barry had calculated the cost of the building were of a most fallacious description'. Such accusations amounted to a charge of fraud but Sir Robert Peel sprang to Barry's defence though he began his speech by lamenting the fact that he had ever allowed himself to be nominated as one of the Commissioners in such a contentious matter. As recorded in *Hansard*:

'a fine picture, well calculated to deceive one young and inexperienced in architecture'

> 'There certainly was one point on which he (Sir Robert Peel) had firmly made up his mind – never again to act as a Commissioner upon any subject of this kind, where a preference was to be given to the skill of one man as compared with that of others'.

However, he went on to concede that his position was a happy one compared with that of the wretched architect who had actually won the competition:

> '... he would rather be a Commissioner than the successful competitor, to be hunted and pursued with every species of invective in the way that Mr Barry had been'.

The criticism, though seen off by the Government on this occasion, presaged the disputes which were to accompany the completion of the building over the next quarter century, and which caused Barry to suffer much illness and anxiety. In the event the building was to cost almost two and a half times the estimate, thereby establishing a tradition of overspending in parliamentary works which was gloriously reproduced in the parliamentary office building, Portcullis House, two centuries later.

establishing a tradition of overspending in parliamentary works

Augustus Welby Northmore Pugin

In carrying out his designs Barry made use of the services of other professionals of distinction. Work began in July 1837 with the embankment of the river and this work was superintended by James Walker (1781–1862), president of the Institution of Civil Engineers, who had extensive experience of canal and railway work. Piles were sunk in the river enclosing the area to be embanked and the gaps between the piles were filled with a mixture of clay and spoil. The water was then pumped out leaving a dry area, protected from the river, within which the embankment could be built. This technique, and others, would be used on a much greater scale 20 years later by Joseph Bazalgette, when he built the Victoria Embankment.[13]

Earlier in his career, as noted above, Barry had won the competition for the design of the school which became known as King Edward VI, Birmingham, and this work had brought him into contact with two men who were to make major contributions to the new palace. The first was a stonemason called John Thomas, to whom Barry entrusted the design and execution of stone carvings throughout the building. Thomas supervised the team of stonemasons he employed very effectively, and no controversy arose in his relationship with Barry.

The second person was Augustus Welby Northmore Pugin, with whom the relationship was more disputatious though the controversy was promoted by Pugin's son, Edward, rather than by the artist himself. Augustus Pugin (1812–52) was the son of the French refugee Auguste de Pugin whom Nash had employed in the 1790s in Wales.[14] The son, who, like Barry, had been educated at Christ's Hospital, was an ardent Catholic and a strong advocate of the Gothic style in both architecture and in decoration, on which subject he had published a

Augustus Welby Northmore Pugin (1812–1852). (By courtesy of the National Portrait Gallery, London)

treatise, *Gothic Furniture*, in 1835. The growing fashion for the Gothic style later brought him so many commissions that he lost his reason from overwork and spent much of the last year of his life in Bedlam. Barry decided to employ Pugin to prepare the detailed drawings for the stained glass windows, wood carvings, metalwork and panelling throughout the palace: a decision which made Pugin's reputation. Pugin also designed the throne. The two men appear to have worked harmoniously together and, although Pugin probably exercised much influence over Barry's designs, the younger man appears to have been perfectly satisfied with the subordinate role publicly credited to him in the design of the building.

he lost his reason from overwork and spent much of the last year of his life in Bedlam

Pugin's son Edward (1834–1875), however, was far from satisfied. Born in the year that the old palace was burned down he can have had no personal recollection of the events that surrounded the submission of Barry's successful design. As his father's mind gave way under the stress of overwork, Edward Pugin found himself prematurely in charge of his father's practice: a formidable challenge for a boy of 17. In 1867, 15 years after his father's death and seven years after Barry's, Edward Pugin published a booklet entitled 'Who was the Art Architect of the Houses of Parliament?'[15] The purpose of the work is clear from the dedication, which is addressed to 'the Lords and Commons':

> '*I earnestly solicit your aid in obtaining for my father the share of fame due to him, as the Art Architect of your Houses of Parliament, which has hitherto been unjustly assigned to another.*'

The work is long-winded, pompous and tendentious

The work is long-winded, pompous and tendentious, and was accompanied by a series of letters which Pugin wrote to *The Times* and the *Pall Mall Gazette*[16]. He claimed that his father had 'made the sections and working drawings for every portion of the building' and that these drawings had then been copied by Charles Barry and submitted in his own hand as his own work. Unwisely he wrote that his claims would be supported by the testimony of a man called Talbot Bury, who had worked both with his father and with Pugin. Talbot Bury felt otherwise. He asserted that,[17] on the contrary, Barry had been responsible for the design of the building and Pugin for the decorations under Barry's overall guidance. He specifically refuted the charge of plagiarism that was implied in Edward Pugin's claim. The claims of the rival camps were summarised in a publication by Barry's son the following year which, though almost as long-winded as Pugin's, leaves little room for doubt on the matter. Barry was the principal designer with much valuable, acknowledged assistance from

Augustus Pugin (and John Thomas, whose descendants were presumably less nervous or contentious).[18]

Delays and complaints

The 'Pugin controversy' did not worry Barry during his lifetime but he had plenty of other anxieties to distract him. The first concerned a continuous flow of complaints from members of both houses of Parliament about the progress of the construction work and features of the design. One of the first to complain was Lord Brougham, a former member of Melbourne's government. Brougham objected to the inclusion of a Ladies' Gallery in Barry's design, declaring 'I think the ladies would be better employed in almost any other way, than in attending parliamentary debates … he wished always to see them in their proper places', the clear implication that 'their proper places' did not include the Houses of Parliament.

More serious problems followed as factions within Parliament set up a series of supervisory committees whose ostensible purpose was to check on the execution of the work but who often competed with one another. Thus during the construction of the new palace the Commons were accommodated within a temporary structure on the site of the former Court of Requests. The Commons were well satisfied with this arrangement because their new, temporary accommodation was more comfortable and spacious than their former home in St Stephen's Chapel. The Lords were not happy because they were despatched to cramped quarters on the site of the former painted chamber. In 1844 they set up a Lords Committee to enquire into delays to the work and into changes to the design which had allegedly been made by Barry as the work progressed. The architect was obliged to make numerous appearances before this and other committees and was eventually exonerated. Most of the alterations to the design had been authorised by the Commissioners and those that had not were minor items of detail sanctioned by normal architectural practice. Barry became ill as a result of the extra work and anxiety occasioned by such enquiries, though he must have drawn some consolation from the letter written to him by Lord de Grey, whose position as first president of the Society of British Architects (later the Royal Institute of British Architects) no doubt made him more sympathetic to Barry than were most of his fellow peers. On 3 June 1850 he wrote to Barry:

> 'Sir Christopher Wren had to deal with men who knew what they wanted … I am sorry to say that august assembly which has most to do with the erection of this magnificent structure has in it a vast number of men who

'I think the ladies would be better employed in almost any other way, than in attending parliamentary debates … he wished always to see them in their proper places'

ask questions, make suggestions and offer criticisms,
while at the same time they do not know what is wanted
or, indeed, what they want themselves'.[19]

A matter of payment

This letter was written specifically in connection with a controversy
which was to dog the whole project, causing Barry much distress and
leaving him out of pocket. The fact that the commissioners did not feel
themselves 'called upon to make the cost of any design an object of our
consideration', referred to above, did not mean that their generosity
would extend to the architect. On the contrary. The parsimonious
attitude to public expenditure which had been suspended in the design
and construction of the building which would have the honour of
being occupied by the Lords and Commons was reinstated in double
measure in the matter of the architect's fee.

It was normal professional practice at the time for the architect's fee
to be set at 5 percent of the cost of construction. This arrangement
meant that, if costs escalated as a result of changes made to the
specification by clients, the extra work for the architect earned further
fees. As the work progressed the various supervisory committees
referred to above did indeed impose a number of extra requirements
on their distracted architect. The most demanding, concerning the
heating and ventilation system and the famous clock, are described
below. As a result the cost of the building eventually mounted to
£1,997,246,[20] a figure which would have earned Barry a fee of almost
£100,000. In March 1839 the Treasury, possibly alarmed by the
already growing costs of the project, wrote to Barry announcing that
they would pay him a fee of £25,000 for the design. Given that the
work had been underway for almost two years, with no previous
intimation that the Treasury would depart from normal practice, this
came as a most unpleasant surprise to Barry, who was struggling to
keep up with the demands for drawings while neglecting his normal
practice of much more profitable commercial work.

He then engaged in a fruitless correspondence with the Treasury
which dragged on for 20 years. His letters were often unanswered.
The Treasury refused Barry's offer of arbitration and was not above
leaking correspondence to *The Times* if it helped its case. In one such
leak the Lords of the Treasury revealed that they had offered a fee of
3 percent, with some extras on top of that and 'as far as they are
concerned they must record these terms as their final decision'. Barry
replied that their lordships had 'constituted themselves the judges in
their own case' and that they were paying the normal 5 percent
commission on other projects.[21] The Council of the Royal Institute of

British Architects supported Barry, declaring that the Treasury's attitude was 'disastrous to the future prospects of architecture as a liberal profession in this country and unworthy of the government of a great nation'. The rhetoric achieved nothing. Barry may have built his reputation on his role as architect of the Palace of Westminster but he certainly didn't build a fortune. It cost him money.

Heat, light and ventilation

Barry's next ordeal concerned the arrangements for heating, lighting and ventilating the building and in this, as in other matters, he was surrounded by advisers whose opinions were stronger than their understanding. Members of both Houses held strong views because the arrangements in the former palace had been far from satisfactory. Over the next few years, therefore, no less than seven select committees were established on lighting, ventilating and warming the building, four by the Commons and three by the Lords.[22] This proliferation of committees reflected different views of the mechanisms that should be adopted to deal with the matters, differences which were to haunt Charles Barry for more than a decade. A Commons Committee was impressed by the representations of a medical practitioner, Dr David Reid, who had written a book on the subject and proposed to ventilate the building by means of one shaft through a central tower by which all smoke and air would be discharged from the building. This was an attractive suggestion since it would dispense with the need for unsightly chimneys. Reid was appointed in 1840 to oversee the construction of the system for the House of Commons though Barry was left with the Lords: a most unsatisfactory division of responsibility.

As the building work progressed doubts began to emerge. The central tower could become a serious fire hazard, which would expose the building to the same risk as the old palace: that of destruction through the agency of its own heating system. Barry encountered further difficulties in dealing with Reid, as shown in his evidence to a Lords Committee in 1846.[23] First Reid had specified an iron floor for the tower; then he had decided that he preferred a wooden one; then he had put forward seven different designs for the flues to conduct the air and smoke from the building. Reid was evasive and confusing in his evidence, perhaps attempting to blind his listeners with science; Barry was exasperated, making reference to 'the ingenious attempts made by Dr Reid to mystify the facts'. Their lordships decided that they 'cannot recommend that any expense should be incurred in extending a complicated system of Ventilation to any other parts of the new Building'. Six years later another committee laboured for two months

the Treasury's attitude was 'disastrous to the future prospects of architecture as a liberal profession in this country and unworthy of the government of a great nation' and produced a report, running to 670 pages, which concluded that the heating system 'should be confided to one competent person'.[24]

That person was Goldsworthy Gurney (1793–1885), whom we have met before, trying out his steam-powered carriage from his new house in Nash's Regent's Park.[25] His credentials were more impressive than those of Dr Reid. Gurney worked more harmoniously with Barry, though he had some anxious moments. In June 1858 the hot, dry summer reached its climax and the stench from the sewage in the Thames was such that the press named the crisis 'The Great Stink'. Rooms overlooking the Thames in the almost-completed building had to be abandoned by members who were unable to stand the smell. Gurney wrote to the Speaker that, in the circumstances, he could 'no longer be responsible for the health of the house'.[26] This provoked a debate, the outcome of which was Bazalgette's construction of London's main drainage.[27]

in the circumstances, he could 'no longer be responsible for the health of the house'

The great clock

Barry's difficulties in constructing the heating system were as nothing compared with those he encountered in building the great clock. The building of the clocktower had begun in 1843 and Barry had arranged for the clock to be designed by Benjamin Vulliamy (1780–1854), Master of the Clockmakers Company and a personal friend. One of the three Parliamentary Committees that deliberated upon the matter decided that a competition should be held for the design and

SIR GOLDSWORTHY GURNEY, 1793-1885

A Cornishman by birth, Goldsworthy Gurney practised as a surgeon in Wadebridge before moving to London in 1820 where he delivered lectures on chemistry which impressed the young Michael Faraday. Gurney developed the process for producing limelight, the very bright light which is used in theatrical productions; the blowtorch; and a steam jet which was used by the Stephensons in *The Rocket*. Gurney also patented a steam carriage which he exercised in Regent's Park before travelling in it from London to Bath and back in 1829 at an average speed of 15mph. He was given responsibility for installing the lighting and heating system in the Palace of Westminster, a task which caused great anxiety to himself and to the increasingly harassed Charles Barry. (Picture by courtesy of the National Portrait Gallery, London)

manufacture of the clock, the judge to be Sir George Airy (1801–92), the Astronomer Royal. Airy dismissed Vulliamy's proposed design as 'a village clock of very superior character'. He specified that the clock should be accurate to within one second in any hour. He awarded the job of designing it to Edmund Beckett Denison (1806–1905) and that of making it to Edward Dent (1790–1853). Dent was a clockmaker of distinction who designed the clock for the Great Exhibition of 1851 (later installed at King's Cross Station) and the clock for the Royal Exchange.

Denison was a different matter. He had been born Edmund Beckett, son of a Yorkshire baronet. The father had adopted the name Denison, which the son discarded before being created 1st Baron Grimthorpe for his contributions to church architecture. His entry in the *Dictionary of National Biography* gives some clue to the nature of the problems that he posed for Barry. He is described as 'lawyer, mechanician and controversialist'. His appetite for controversy outshone his other qualities. He had written extensively on church architecture and had designed churches in his native Yorkshire. His early career as a controversialist, marked by his 'powers of sarcasm and assertive manner',[28] was exercised on behalf of the Protestant cause in opposition to the ritualism which had entered the Church of England as a result of the Oxford Movement.

George Airy. (By courtesy of the National Portrait Gallery, London)

The Houses of Parliament. (By courtesy of the Guildhall Library, Corporation of London)

EDMUND BECKETT DENISON, 1ST BARON GRIMTHORPE, (1816–1905)

Edmund Beckett was born in Yorkshire and educated at Eton and Trinity College, Cambridge, where he studied mathematics before becoming a barrister. He succeeded to his father's baronetcy in 1874. He devoted his life to the study of astronomy, clock making and architecture, particularly Gothic architecture as applied to church buildings. He was a man of firm views which left no room for the views of others. His role in the construction of the parliamentary clock is described elsewhere. In 1877 he descended upon St Albans Abbey. Since the Reformation the abbey had fallen into disrepair, but its promotion to the status of cathedral of the new diocese of St Albans in that year had led to the formation of a committee to restore it. The members had difficulty raising the necessary funds so in 1877 Beckett obtained a faculty from the new diocese to 'restore, repair and refit' the abbey at his own expense. His restoration, which followed his own theories of architecture, is still a subject of controversy, since he imposed some unmistakeably Victorian notions on a building whose construction had commenced in the reign of William the Conqueror using Roman bricks. Nevertheless, without Beckett's work the building might not have survived at all. He became 1st Baron Grimthorpe in 1886 for his services to the church.

In 1850 Beckett had written *A Rudimentary Treatise on Clock and Watch Making* following a lengthy study of the subject and had designed the clock made by Dent for the Great Exhibition. This had earned him the friendship of Airy, though that friendship did not long survive Airy's attempt to work with Beckett on the parliamentary clock. Some idea of his character may be gained by examining his relationship with the Horological Institute. In 1868 the members elected him as their president in recognition of his undoubted technical achievements in the field but they wisely stipulated, as a condition of his election, that he be forbidden to attend their dinners in order to avoid the arguments that would otherwise be sure to follow.

they wisely stipulated, as a condition of his election, that he be forbidden to attend their dinners

Barry, who was charged with building the tower which would house the clock, tried vainly to extract from Beckett and Dent the information he needed on the size and character of the mechanism and the bells that he had to accommodate. Beckett, who could never see any point of view but his own, wrote a series of offensive letters to and about Barry. After he had written to *The Times* referring to 'the stupidity of Sir C. Barry' the newspaper declined to print any more of his correspondence. The clock mechanism was completed in 1855 but Barry now had to wait for the bells. In the words of Barry's son, 'much discussion took place on whether the tower was waiting for the clock, or the clock waiting for the tower'. In 1856, tired of waiting, and worried that rainwater would damage the inside of the tower, Barry installed a temporary roof and awaited the resolution of the saga of the bells. Within the tower he had incorporated the prison cells specified in the original design for persons showing disrespect to Parliament. The last occupant was the suffragette, Mrs Emmeline Pankhurst, who was confined there in 1902.

The first great bell, to sound the hours, was cast in 1856 in Stockton by a company called Warner of Cripplegate. It weighed 16 tons and was hoisted into place later that year, accompanied by the clock mechanism. Warner had specified that the clapper should not exceed seven hundredweight. Beckett thought he knew better and insisted on a clapper weighing 13 hundredweight. This caused the bell to crack. The clock was then removed, together with the great bell. It was recast by the Whitechapel foundry and reinstalled, weighing 13½ tons, in 1859. In the meantime the clock's hands had been redesigned twice. The original weight was such that they fell from 12 o'clock to 6 o'clock and struggled back up the clockface to 12 o'clock. The clock was commissioned on 31 May 1859. However, the saga had not quite finished. The great bell cracked again in September 1859. It was repaired in situ but the crack remains there to this day. Some controversy surrounds the naming of the bell. Strictly speaking it is the great bell itself which is called 'Big Ben', though the name has come to be attached to both the clock as a whole and to the tower (St Stephen's Tower) which houses it. A contemporary tradition held that the name 'Big Ben' was suggested facetiously during a Commons debate involving the lofty Sir Benjamin Hall, Commissioner of Works, who had set up the committee which designed the bell, though there is no record of this in *Hansard*. Another tradition suggests that the name was derived from that of Ben Caunt, an 18-stone boxer of formidable reputation whose retirement from the ring coincided with the installation of the bell. The clock has always been extremely accurate, old penny pieces being added to or removed from the mechanism, each one accelerating or retarding the mechanism by two-fifths of a second. Until 1913 the mechanism was wound manually once a week, two

'much discussion took place on whether the tower was waiting for the clock, or the clock waiting for the tower'

The great bell cracked again in September 1859

A contemporary tradition held that the name 'Big Ben' was suggested facetiously during a Commons debate

SIR BENJAMIN HALL, 1802-67

An early campaigner for the Welsh language, the Welshman Benjamin Hall sat as MP first for Monmouth and later for Marylebone. In 1838 he became a baronet and in 1859 Baron Llanover. A vigorous parliamentary campaigner, he directed his energies against the abuse of election expenses and against sinecures in the Church of England. He ousted Edwin Chadwick from the Board of Health in 1854 and effectively excluded him from further public office. In 1855 he became Chief Commissioner of Works, in which capacity he was responsible for delaying Joseph Bazalgette's great works to provide London with effective sewers;[29] and for supervising the later stages of the rebuilding of the Palace of Westminster after the conflagration of 1834. A tall, imposing man, he has a strong claim to having given his name to 'Big Ben', the principal bell in the new parliamentary clock.

men taking 32 hours to complete the task. In that year a winding mechanism was installed in their place.

The Lords had occupied their chamber since 1847 and the Queen opened the building officially in 1852, Charles Barry being awarded a knighthood in the same year. When he died in 1860 the building itself was fully occupied, though the great bell was still being repaired and another three years would pass before Goldsworthy Gurney earned his knighthood for completing the building's heating, lighting and ventilation system. The final stages of the construction were therefore supervised by Barry's son Edward (1830–80).

Sir Charles Barry's final years

In 1853, following the official opening of Parliament, Sir Charles

Barry had retired to a house in Clapham, recently developed by Thomas Cubitt.[30] During the long period that the New Palace of Westminster was being built Barry was engaged in other work in London. He levelled and paved Trafalgar Square and built a terrace on the north side, in front of the National Gallery, in the wall of which are the standard measures for yards, feet and inches. He served on the Great Exhibition building committee which eventually selected Paxton's Crystal Palace to house the exhibition.[31] He designed government buildings in Whitehall, including one for the Treasury and one for the Privy Council, and prepared further designs for the College of Surgeons and Lincoln's Inn. He opposed the ambitious plans for the development of the museums complex in South Kensington, writing to the Prince Consort in October 1853 to argue the case for a 'British Museum of Arts and Literature' in Bloomsbury and only a 'National Gallery

Tower Bridge, the work of Sir John Wolfe-Barry.

of Science' in Kensington.[32] Fortunately for Kensington, and for Alfred Waterhouse, his suggestion was ignored.[33] Following his death on 12 May 1860, he was buried in Westminster Abbey, and a statue of him was erected within the Palace of Westminster itself. The palace was the object of repeated attacks by the Luftwaffe during World War Two and was bombed on 11 occasions between September 1940 and May 1941. On 10 May 1941 the House of Commons was destroyed and the Commons moved into the Lords' Chamber. The destruction was made good in 1945–50 by Sir Giles Gilbert Scott, the work being executed in a style which faithfully followed Barry's original while toning down some of Pugin's more ornate decoration.

Tower Bridge

Like Isambard Kingdom Brunel earlier in the century, John Wolfe-Barry (1836–1918) followed his father by making his own distinctive addition to the skyline of Victorian London. He was Barry's youngest son and added the name Wolfe to his surname in 1898 in recognition of his father's lifelong close friendship with John Wolfe. He became a civil engineer and worked with Sir John Hawkshaw (1811–91) on the design and construction of Charing Cross and Cannon Street Stations; on the District Railway extension to Ealing; the East London Railway, through Brunel's Thames Tunnel;[34] and on the completion of the Inner Circle between Whitechapel and Aldgate. He later built the Surrey commercial docks east of Tower Bridge. However, his most conspicuous monument is Tower Bridge itself.

A proposal for a crossing east of London Bridge had been made as early as 1879 by Sir Joseph Bazalgette, Chief Engineer to the Metropolitan Board of Works.[35] The problem with such a bridge was that it would have to be built in a way that enabled ships to gain access to the upper pool of London, east of London Bridge itself, which at that time was the world's busiest port. Either the bridge had to be high enough for ships to pass beneath it or it would have to be designed to enable ships to pass through it. Bazalgette's proposal was for a bridge with a clearance of 65 feet, to be reached by a long, sloping gradient starting at the Royal Mint on the north side and by a spiral approach on the south side. The City authorities regarded the proposed clearance as inadequate for the tallest ships at high tide and preferred a design by their own architect, (from 1886 Sir) Horace Jones (1819–87). Jones proposed an arched 'bascule' design: a bridge that could be raised to admit ships to the upper pool and lowered to enable traffic to cross. There were flaws in his design which John Wolfe-Barry was enlisted to correct. Working with Jones, he replaced Jones's arch with a horizontal pedestrian walkway and designed the mechanism which would enable the bridge to be raised and lowered, giving a clearance of 135 feet. In this John Wolfe-Barry was assisted by a young engineer called Henry Marc Brunel, son of Isambard and grandson of Marc Brunel. In 1881 the foundation stone was laid and the famous bridge was opened in a great ceremony by the Prince of Wales on 30 June, 1894.

Many buildings and a few objects can claim to represent London in the minds of visitors. They would include Buckingham Palace, the Tower of London, Harry Beck's famous schematic map of the London

Underground, Trafalgar Square and Piccadilly Circus. Yet none would have a greater claim than the New Palace of Westminster and Tower Bridge, the works of Sir Charles Barry and son.

[1] *Memoir of the Life and Works of the Late Sir Charles Barry, Architect*, by Dr Alfred Barry, John Murray, 1870, page 7.

[2] See Chapter 8 for a description of Waterhouse's experiences and impressions.

[3] *Memoir of the Life and Works of the Late Sir Charles Barry, Architect*, by Dr Alfred Barry, John Murray, 1870, page 22.

[4] *On the Architectural Career of Sir Charles Barry*, a lecture by Sir Matthew Digby Wyatt at the Royal Institute of British Architects, 21 May, 1860; page 4; British Library ref. 10825.f.14.

[5] *Memoir of the Life and Works of the Late Sir Charles Barry, Architect*, by Dr Alfred Barry, John Murray, 1870, page 68, note.

[6] See Chapter 6 for an account of 'The Great Stink'.

[7] Parliamentary papers 1835, volume 18, *Report of the Select Committee on Rebuilding the Houses of Parliament*.

[8] Parliamentary papers 1836, paper 374, *Report of Commissioners appointed by His Majesty to examine and Report upon the Plans which might be offered by the competitors for re-building the Houses of Parliament*.

[9] He visited Brussels and Louvain and probably several other cities at the same time.

[10] See Chapter 8.

[11] *On the Architectural Career of Sir Charles Barry*, a lecture by Sir Matthew Digby Wyatt at the Royal Institute of British Architects, 21 May 1860; page 7; British Library ref. 10825.f.14.

[12] *Hansard*, volume 35, columns 399–415, 21 July 1836.

[13] See Chapter 6 for an account of Bazalgette's work.

[14] See Chapter 1 for an account of Nash's work.

[15] *Who was the Art Architect of the Houses of Parliament?*, by Edward Welby Pugin, Longmans Green, 1867.

[16] *The Times*, 7 September 1867, page 11; *Pall Mall Gazette*, 13 and 27 August 1867.

[17] *Pall Mall Gazette*, 19 August 1867.

[18] *The Architect of the new Palace at Westminster. A reply to a pamphlet by E.W. Pugin, Esq.* by Alfred Barry, John Murray, 1868.

[19] *On the Architectural Career of Sir Charles Barry*, a lecture by Sir Matthew Digby Wyatt at the Royal Institute of British Architects, 21 May 1860; page 11; British Library ref. 10825.f.14.

[20] *Memoir of the Life and Works of the Late Sir Charles Barry, Architect*, by Dr Alfred Barry, John Murray, 1870, page 229.

[21] *The Times* 15 February 1856, page 10; Barry's reply was published on 18 February, page 10.

[22] *General Index to Parliamentary papers*, 1801–52, lists them all.

[23] *Parliamentary papers*, 1846, volume 14; Barry's evidence was heard on 23 February and 14 August.

[24] *Parliamentary papers*, 1852, volume 16.

[25] See Chapter 1.

[26] *Hansard*, 1857–8, volume 151, column 23, 25 June 1858.

[27] See Chapter 6 for an account of 'The Great Stink' and Bazalgette's work.

[28] *Dictionary of National Biography*, 1901–11, Oxford University Press, page 121.

[29] See Chapter 6 for an account of 'The Great Stink'.

[30] See Chapter 3 for an account of Thomas Cubitt's development of Clapham.

[31] See Chapter 4 for an account of Paxton's work.

[32] *Memoir of the Life and Works of the Late Sir Charles Barry, Architect*, by Dr Alfred Barry, John Murray, 1870, page 358.

[33] See Chapter 8 for an account of Waterhouse's Natural History Museum.

[34] See Chapter 2 for an account of Brunel's Thames Tunnel.

[35] See Chapter 6 for an account of Bazalgette's work in London on this and other matters.

CHAPTER 6

Sir Joseph Bazalgette and the Cleansing of Victorian London

'This superb and far-sighted engineer probably did more good, and saved more lives, than any single Victorian public official.'[1]

'It is two years since the most extensive and wonderful work of modern times was commenced, and yet the inhabitants of this metropolis seem to take little interest in the undertaking'
(*The Observer*, 14 April, 1861, describing Bazalgette's work in London)

Joseph Bazalgette as Chief Engineer to the Metropolitan Board of Works, about 1865. (Thames Water plc)

THESE quotations refer to the great engineering works of Sir Joseph Bazalgette (1819–91) who, by designing and building a comprehensive system of sewers, pumping stations and treatment works, turned the Thames from an open sewer and source of epidemic disease into one of the cleanest metropolitan rivers in the world, which it remains. Yet the quotations, flattering though they are, fail to do full justice to the achievement of an engineer who did much else besides, building more of London than anyone else before or since. He created famous streets, three embankments, three bridges across the Thames, a ferry service and many parks and other open spaces. Like the sewers, these all remain in use and their excellent condition is a testimony to the thoroughness with which they were designed and built.

Who was Sir Joseph Bazalgette?

Bazalgette, like his friend and contemporary Isambard Kingdom Brunel, was of French descent. His grandfather, Jean Louis Bazalgette, was born in 1750 at Ispagnac, in France, close to the remote hamlet of La Bazalgette in the Auvergne, the most thinly populated part of France. The origins of the name are obscure. It is unusual even in France. One source suggests that it may derive from the name of the Turkish sultan Bajazet, but there is little beyond hearsay to support this legend. Jean Louis left France in about 1770 and reached England in the late 1770s via the West Indies, where he appears to have made the beginnings of what became a substantial fortune. Jean Louis established himself as a tailor in Mayfair and, perhaps in an attempt to establish himself socially in his new country, proceeded to lend over £20,000 to well-connected people who were better at borrowing money than paying it back. They included the Prince of Wales (the future George IV), three of the Prince's brothers and one of his friends, the playwright Sheridan. Parliamentary Commissioners charged with handling the prince's disorderly finances eventually paid back to Jean Louis most of the money he was owed.[2]

Jean Louis had a son, Joseph William, born in 1783. Joseph entered the Royal Navy and became a sub-lieutenant on 15 October 1805, six days before the battle of Trafalgar. He attended Nelson's funeral. In 1809 he was wounded in an engagement off the Spanish coast and was granted a lifetime pension of £150. His only son, Joseph William the future engineer, was born on 28 March 1819. At the age of 17 he was articled to the civil engineer Sir John MacNeill, who had himself been one of the principal assistants of Thomas Telford in building roads and bridges. Bazalgette learned his engineering by working under MacNeill's guidance and by joining the Institution of Civil Engineers, where he and his fellow members read papers to one another on new materials, techniques and problems. In 1842 he set up his own civil engineering practice in Great George Street, off Parliament Square. This was the 'Harley Street' of the engineering profession, close to the site of the Institution of Civil Engineers itself. A period of frantic activity on railway projects was followed by a breakdown in Bazalgette's health following which he entered public service.

'The whole of the river was an opaque, pale brown fluid'

While Bazalgette was learning his trade the Thames was turning into a sewer. In mediaeval times sewage was collected in cesspools which

Jean Louis proceeded to lend over £20,000 to well-connected people who were better at borrowing money than paying it back

were to be found in the basements of houses. At intervals these were emptied, at night, by 'nightsoilmen' who shovelled out the contents, loaded it on to carts and sold it as fertiliser to farmers. The trade continued into the 20th century. As late as 1904 the Grand Union Canal company was conveying on barges 45,669 tons of this manure to be applied to the Hertfordshire countryside. There was a system of sewers beneath the London streets but these were designed only to collect rainwater and empty it into the Thames via the network of substantial rivers like the Fleet, the Westbourne and the Effra, which still run beneath the capital, most of them now completely covered by buildings and streets. The most visible of these lost rivers is the

THOMAS CRAPPER & CO.'S
Sanitary Specialities,

IMPROVED
LAVATORY BASIN.

	£	s.	d.
White Ware, fitted with combined Overflow and Waste, and ½ Standard Screw-down Valves ...	2	19	6
Plated Fittings, Extra	0	8	6

ELASTIC VALVE CLOSET.

No. 78.—Valve Closet, with white china dish with gold lines, and handle, white ware flushing rim basin, 1 in. supply valve, copper air regulator, complete as shown.

		£3	9	6
If with 1¼ in. valve	Extra	0	3	6
„ Ornamental Basin	„	0	3	6
„ White and Gold Basin	„	0	8	9
„ Box Enamelled inside	„	0	4	9
„ Box fitted with Brass Top ...	„	0	6	3
„ Box fitted with union to connect Ventilating Pipe	„	0	3	9
„ 4 in. outlet	„	0	7	9

IMPROVED SYPHON
Water Waste Preventer.

	£	s.	d.
Cast-Iron 2 Gallon Syphon Waste Preventer, with Tranquil Inlet Valve, and Silencing Air Tubes, and Brass Chain and China Pull	1	1	6
Ditto, 3 gallon ditto	1	3	6

50, 52, & 54, MARLBOROUGH ROAD, CHELSEA, LONDON, S.W.

'A certain flush with every pull'. Thomas Crapper's business traded in Chelsea into the 1960s. Contrary to popular belief his name was a fortunate coincidence, the word 'crap' having been in use since Shakespeare's time.

Westbourne, which rises on Hampstead Heath, surfaces in central London in the form of the Serpentine in Hyde Park and crosses Sloane Square underground station in the form of a culvert which passes above the trains. The cesspool system worked well until the late 18th century, the nightsoilmen being very well paid for this smelly but dependable occupation.

the real culprit was the water-closet

In the early 19th century the system started to break down in the face of three problems. London's population grew from less than a million in 1801 to almost two and a half million by 1850. Areas which had been farmland in the late 18th century, like St Pancras, were now covered by houses, factories and railway stations. The fields retreated as the inhabited area increased. The nightsoilmen had to travel much further, at greater cost, to dispose of their manure. The second factor was guano, solidified bird droppings which, from 1847, was imported from South America and sold as a richer and more manageable fertiliser. However, the real culprit was the water-closet. It had been invented in the 16th century by Sir John Harington, but he only made two: one for himself and one for his godmother, Queen Elizabeth I. In the late 18th century a Yorkshire carpenter called Joseph Bramah had redesigned the WC so that it was much easier to mass-produce. It rapidly became a desirable feature of every middle-class home and its position as a status symbol was enhanced when an enterprising manufacturer called George Jennings installed some of his closets at the Great Exhibition of 1851, where 827,000 visitors used the device for the first time.

'a certain flush with every pull'

In 1861 Thomas Crapper opened a competitive business in Chelsea, marketing his products under the memorable slogan 'a certain flush

JOSEPH BRAMAH (1748–1814)

Joseph Bramah, the son of a Yorkshire farmer, was one of the most prolific inventors there has ever been, registering 18 patents. His name was originally spelt Bramma. After apprenticeship to a carpenter he travelled to London to start his own business. In 1778 he was engaged to install a water-closet in a private house and realised that he could improve the design so that it would both work better and be easier to mass-produce. He patented the new mechanism (changing the spelling of his name in the process) and started to manufacture WCs in large numbers. Their widespread adoption was largely responsible for the crisis in 19th-century London which became known as 'The Great Stink' of 1858. He also invented an unpickable lock and offered a prize of £200 to anyone who could pick it. The prize was eventually claimed by an American called Hobbs who took up the challenge at the Great Exhibition of 1851, long after Bramah's death. Bramah's other inventions included a hydraulic press, an ever-pointed pencil, a machine for numbering banknotes and an early screw mechanism for propelling ships.

with every pull'. By 1857 it was estimated that 200,000 WCs had been installed in London.

The connection of the new water-closets to antiquated cesspools had disastrous consequences. Every time a closet was flushed a small amount of potential manure was sent into the cesspool, accompanied by 10 or 20 times the volume of water. The cesspools filled up correspondingly quickly with liquid which was of no interest to farmers and which could be relied upon to leak into surrounding watercourses. When they didn't leak they overflowed. The social reformer Edwin Chadwick recorded the experience of an engineer called Howell who had inspected two houses in the 1840s:

> 'I found whole areas of the cellars of both houses were full of nightsoil, to the depth of three feet, which had been permitted to accumulate for years from the overflow of the cesspools ... I found the yard covered in nightsoil, from the overflowing of the privy to the depth of nearly six inches and bricks were placed to enable the inmates to get across dryshod'.[3]

an ever-swelling flow of sewage passed not into cesspools but into the River Thames

The reaction of the authorities was to remove the prohibition on connecting house drains to the public sewers. In 1815 householders were permitted to connect their cesspools and closets to the public sewers; an Act of 1847 *obliged* them to do so. From these dates an ever-swelling flow of sewage passed not into cesspools but into the River Thames via house drains, street sewers and the underground river system. The result was recorded by the scientist Michael Faraday during a journey on the river in the summer of 1855. He wrote to *The Times*:[4]

> 'The appearance and the smell of the water forced themselves at once upon my attention. The whole of the river was an opaque, pale brown fluid ... The smell was very bad. If we neglect this subject we cannot expect to do so with impunity, nor ought we to be surprised if, ere many years are over, a hot season gives us sad proof of the folly of our carelessness'.

The hot season arrived three years later, in 1858. In the meantime over 30,000 Londoners had died in cholera epidemics caused by drinking water polluted by Thames sewage.

The Great Stink

In 1848 a Metropolitan Sewers Commission had been established with

---

SIR EDWIN CHADWICK (1800–90)

Edwin Chadwick's zeal as a campaigner for praiseworthy philanthropic causes was matched only by his capacity for antagonising others who shared his aims and could have been allies. He campaigned for the reform of the Poor Law and became Secretary to the Poor Law Commission, a position he used with ruthless ingenuity to whip into line local Poor Law Guardians who did not approach their tasks with sufficient vigour. The Commission was dissolved as a result of the antagonism his activities aroused. He then turned his attention to the cause of sanitary reform and in 1848 he became a member of the General Board of Health and the Metropolitan Sewers Commission. The following year he (and his principal antagonist) were removed by the Home Secretary from the Metropolitan Sewers Commission in order to bring peace to that body. This left more time for Chadwick to use his position on the General Board of Health to interfere with the work of local boards and this was one of the factors that led first to Chadwick's removal from the Board and then to its abolition. Chadwick never held public office again. He was knighted in 1889, the year before his death.

---

the task of designing and constructing a comprehensive sewerage system which would protect the Thames, and its water supply, from the waste of the population. Over the next seven years a series of commissions split into factions which quarrelled furiously over the appropriate design. In 1849 Bazalgette joined the Commission as an assistant engineer and in 1852 he became chief engineer, his predecessor having died in office from 'harassing fatigues and anxieties of official duties'. In 1855 the Commissioners were replaced by the Metropolitan Board of Works. This was London's first metropolitan Government, with authority to execute construction projects throughout the metropolis covering roads, bridges, parks and, above all, sewers. One of the first acts of the new Board was to appoint Bazalgette as chief engineer. No doubt his familiarity with the plans of the earlier commissions helped him to secure the post but his credentials were also strengthened by the quality of the referees who supported his application. These included the celebrated railway engineer Robert Stephenson, MP, and the even more famous Isambard Kingdom Brunel.

Within five months of his appointment Bazalgette submitted a comprehensive plan for a system of main sewers. They would run

Michael Faraday presenting his card to Father Thames, *Punch*, July 1855. The picture followed Faraday's letter to *The Times* describing the horrors of a journey by boat along the stinking river.

parallel to the river on both sides and intercept the contents of street sewers and house drains before they reached the hidden rivers or the Thames. The intercepting sewers would then conduct the effluent, by gravity, to treatment works at Barking on the north side of the river and Crossness on the south. Four pumping stations were built to lift the sewage into the treatment works. Initially Bazalgette planned to discharge the sewage into the Thames at high tide so that its initial movement would be out to sea, but before he retired he modified the system so that the solid matter was collected in settlement tanks, loaded on to sludge boats, and dumped in the North Sea. This system remained in use until 1998 when it was replaced by incinerators.

There now followed a delay of over two years while Bazalgette's proposals were evaluated by the Government in the person of Sir Benjamin Hall, First Commissioner of Works. Hall, a tall imposing

This system remained in use until 1998

Bazalgette's
intercepting system;
still in use, with later
additions as London
grew.

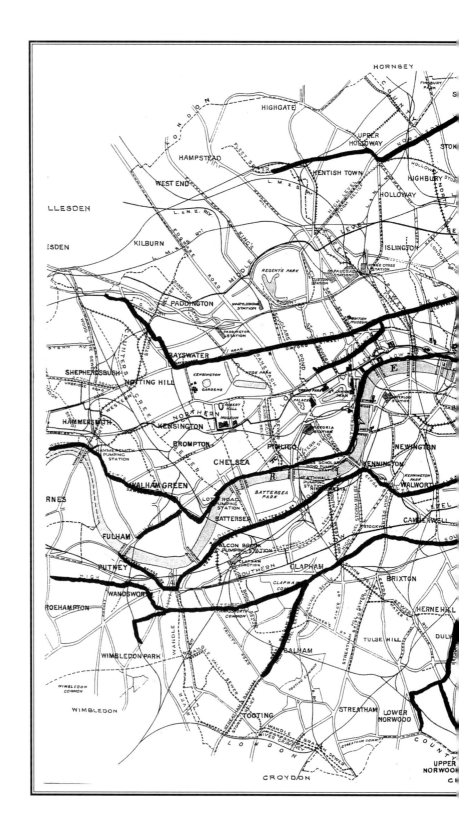

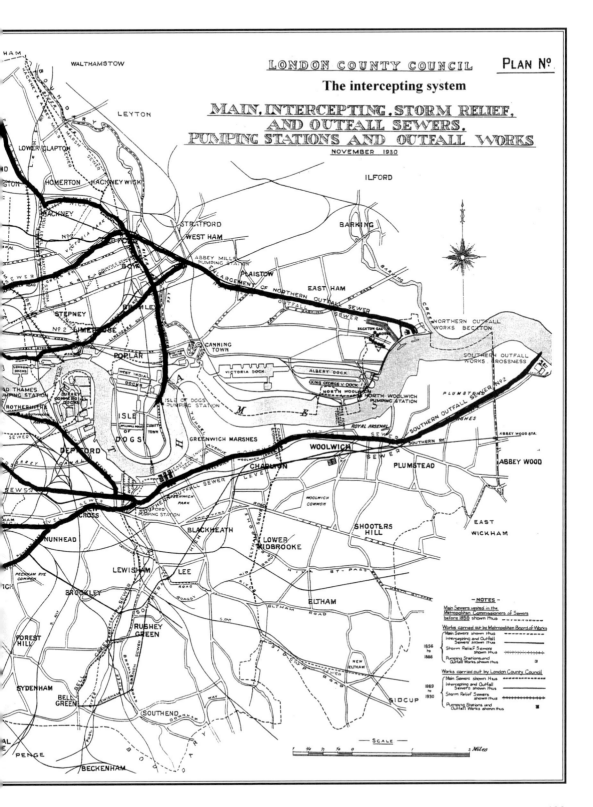

man, had recently overseen the rebuilding of the new Houses of Parliament and had been rewarded for his diligence by supposedly having the great bell of the parliamentary clock named in his honour: Big Ben.[5] Bazalgette's sewers were a greater problem. There followed a long and often ill-tempered argument about whether the system was adequate for the task and, above all, over who should pay for it. The debate was resolved only by the hot, dry summer of 1858 when the stench from the Thames was described in *Hansard*, which recorded the following complaint from an MP on 7 June:[6]

> *'It was a notorious fact that Hon. Gentlemen sitting in the Committee rooms and in the Library were utterly unable to remain there in consequence of the stench which arose from the river'.*

Eleven days later *The Times* recorded its satisfaction with this state of affairs:

> *'A few members, bent upon investigating the matter to its very depth, ventured into the Library, but they were instantaneously driven to retreat, each man with a handkerchief to his nose. We are heartily glad of it'.*

The writer was pleased because he thought that the discomfiture of the parliamentarians would break the deadlock over Bazalgette's plan. He was right. In 18 days Benjamin Disraeli, as Leader of the House, put a Bill through Parliament which removed the Government's veto and authorised the Metropolitan Board of Works to levy rates and borrow money to pay for the construction of Bazalgette's system.

'The most extensive and wonderful work of modern times'.

Bazalgette now began to build 82 miles of main intercepting sewers to run parallel to the Thames and over 1,100 miles of subsidiary sewers to protect the smaller, underground streams. Work began in 1858 and took 17 years to complete. The diagram on pages 132–133 shows the routes of the intercepting sewers, three to the north of the river and two to the south, with branches. In places these sewers are larger than the underground train tunnels. Starting in the north, south and west they conduct the sewage by gravity at a minimum fall of two feet per mile. Four huge pumping stations were built to raise the sewage where it had fallen below the level of the river. The sewers had to cross a dense network of roads, rivers, railways and canals, some of which had to be raised, lowered or rerouted to allow the sewers to follow their

these sewers are larger than the underground train tunnels

steady course. The northern outfall sewer, which collected the northern sewage at Abbey Mills, near West Ham, and conducted it to the treatment works at Barking, was a particularly hazardous task. It was built across a swamp and required the construction of a temporary cement works and railway to provide the great quantities of material required and to convey them to the site. One railway had to be lowered and five roads raised to enable this sewer to pass. Special bricks called Staffordshire Blues were used in the lower part of the sewer to withstand the constant flow of sewage over centuries. A new material, Portland cement, was used to hold the bricks together. Portland cement had been invented years earlier and was known to become harder over time when immersed in water. However, the quality control procedures of the manufacturers were poor and it had acquired a reputation for unreliability. Bazalgette changed that. He had his own men on site, testing every batch to destruction, and ordered that any which failed the test 'shall be peremptorily rejected and forthwith removed from the works'.[7] Manufacturers quickly learned that supplying poor quality cement to Bazalgette was unwise. They installed their own quality assurance procedures and the material quickly became accepted as the industry standard, which it remains.

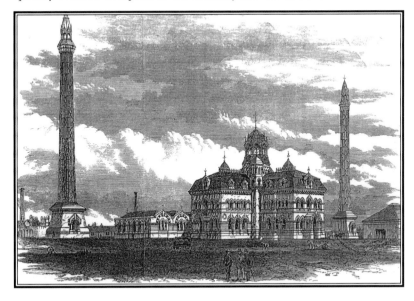

Abbey Mills Pumping Station; West Ham. (*Illustrated London News*)

As the work progressed it received close attention from press and Parliament. *The Observer*, which had originally been sceptical of Bazalgette's plans, wrote in 1861:

'It is two years since the most extensive and wonderful work of modern times was commenced, and yet the

'To Mr Bazalgette no tribute of praise can be undeserved' and a Member of Parliament proposed that he be paid a special bounty of £6,000.[9]

Aerial photograph of Crossness sewage treatment works, with Beckton in the background. The largest treatment works in Europe, it is now operated by Thames Water plc. (Thames Water plc)

inhabitants of this metropolis seem to take little interest in the undertaking.'[8]

The newspaper later declared, with unconscious humour 'Every penny spent is spent in a good cause'. Bazalgette was singled out for particular praise. The normally astringent *Marylebone Mercury* commented 'To Mr Bazalgette no tribute of praise can be undeserved' and a Member of Parliament proposed that he be paid a special bounty of £6,000 for the excellence of his work.[9] Opposition from ratepayers put an end to this suggestion but it is a reflection both of the excellence of the work and the importance attached to it.

Put to the test

The system was commissioned in stages. In April 1865, the southern system came into operation and from that date those living south of the river were free of polluted water. The northern system was not completed until 1868 and in the meantime, 1866, there was one final cholera epidemic. It was confined to Whitechapel, one of the few areas not yet connected to Bazalgette's system. 5,596 people died in an area of a few square miles, where drinking water had been contaminated by

sewage. Finally, in 1875, a small area in the vicinity of Fulham was connected to the system and it was complete. The new facilities were severely tested on 26 July 1867. In nine hours over three inches of rain fell, about one-eighth of the average for a full year. Bazalgette's pumping stations, working at full capacity, had to lift twice the volume of water they were designed to handle. They coped. After that Bazalgette, and Victorian London, knew they had a system in which they could have complete confidence.[10]

The Prince of Wales opening the Metropolitan main drainage works at Crossness, April 1865. (*Illustrated London News*)

The epidemic that didn't happen

In 1892, the year after Bazalgette's death, cholera struck Hamburg, one of London's principal trading partners. Previous epidemics had always arrived by sea, when sick passengers brought the disease ashore. The Government set up a committee to deal with the forthcoming epidemic. There was no epidemic. Seventeen deaths were recorded in London, mostly among arrivals who had contracted the disease abroad.[11]

The system built by Bazalgette remains in use in the 21st century, the only exceptions being very short sections which have been rerouted to accommodate other subterranean works such as underground railways. The system has been enlarged and added to as London has grown. The Thames Water engineers who are responsible for maintaining the sewers report that they are in excellent shape, most of the brickwork being as good as the day it was laid down. There are problems, notably in the branch sewer which runs beneath Piccadilly and collects the outpourings of West End restaurants. When

The Government set up a committee to deal with the forthcoming epidemic

Bazalgette's main sewer, which still serves London after 150 years. (Thames Water plc)

liquid grease and fat hit the cold air of the sewer they solidify and form a thin crust on the sewer walls which has to be removed with water jets and, occasionally, picks and shovels. There is every reason to suppose that the system will last another century at least.

The Victoria Embankment

Bazalgette built much else besides the capital's main drainage. The largest of his great works is the Victoria Embankment, which stretches for over a mile from Westminster Bridge to Blackfriars Bridge. At the latter point it forms a junction with Queen Victoria Street, another of Bazalgette's creations, and thus enables the traveller to pass from the Houses of Parliament to the Bank of England entirely along thoroughfares built by Bazalgette. The Victoria Embankment reclaimed 37 acres of land from the Thames. Its construction was Bazalgette's biggest single work, though the year before his death he told a newspaper 'I get most credit for the Thames Embankment, but it wasn't anything like such a job as the drainage'.[12] Once again the scale of the enterprise required the extensive use of new techniques and materials. A section of the river was sealed off with jetties and a quay and the water pumped out. Portland cement, bricks and other materials were brought in by sailing barge and the construction work

'I get most credit for the Thames Embankment, but it wasn't anything like such a job as the drainage'

proceeded, the relatively new steam shovels supplementing the efforts of labourers in moving the huge quantities of materials required. As always, Bazalgette's inspectors were on site to check materials, reject faulty batches and ensure that the work was being carried out precisely to his specification. When the work was completed the jetties and quay were dismantled and moved along to the next section of the river.

The Victoria Embankment was designed to provide five amenities. First, it was planned to house the low-level intercepting sewer which begins in Hammersmith and runs alongside the Thames for most of its length until it turns north through Limehouse to reach the pumping station at Abbey Mills. This sewer is the last line of defence for the Thames against London's sewage and was one of the largest engineering works of the Victorian period. Without the embankment it would have been necessary to run the sewer along the Strand, Fleet Street and Ludgate Hill, which at that time provided the only route for travellers between Westminster and the City. The congestion on this route was legendary and is celebrated in the contemporary engravings of Gustave Doré. The prospect of adding to the confusion by digging up this thoroughfare did not bear contemplation so, instead of exacerbating the problem, Bazalgette's construction of the embankment added a second amenity by creating a wide, tree-lined thoroughfare beside the Thames which effectively bypassed the congestion. The Prime Minister, Gladstone, was so impressed by Bazalgette's creation that he tried to exploit a loophole in the law which enabled the Crown to claim ownership of the land that

The opening of the Victoria Embankment, 13 July 1870; Somerset House, originally built on the Thames, is now separated from the river by Bazalgette's new structure. (*Illustrated London News*)

Bazalgette had reclaimed from the sewage-laden riverbanks. At this point in his ministry, 1870, Gladstone was still hoping to abolish the income tax which William Pitt had introduced as a 'temporary' measure during the Napoleonic Wars, and he hoped that he would have been assisted in this noble aim by building offices on the embankment and letting them out at commercial rents. The populace, however, was distinctly unappreciative of Gladstone's fiscal rectitude. They wanted the embankment as Bazalgette had planned it, with parks and walkways.

Bazalgette's embankment was saved by the exertions of one of the most under-rated figures of the 19th century: the newspaper-seller, MP and later First Lord of the Admiralty, W.H. Smith (1825–91). In July 1870, Smith proposed in the House of Commons that 'an humble petition be presented to Her Majesty, praying that she will be pleased to direct that no public offices be erected on that portion of the Thames Embankment which is reserved to the Crown, and which has been reclaimed from the river by the ratepayers of the Metropolis'. Gladstone persisted with his claim but *The Times* supported Smith and Bazalgette, referring in a leading article to the condition of the area before Bazalgette's work as 'the worthless foreshore, where dead dogs and cats did mostly congregate ... Like Shylock he [Gladstone] was entitled to his pound of flesh and he clutched it'.[13] A public meeting followed, at St James's Hall, Piccadilly, attended by several hundred ratepayers and Members of Parliament. There was much cheering of Bazalgette and much booing of Gladstone. The Government, ungraciously, abandoned their plans in exchange for a cash payment and a piece of land at the end of Northumberland Avenue (another of Bazalgette's creations) on which the Ministry of Defence now stands. Victoria Embankment Gardens was preserved as a much-needed green space in this busy part of London, thus creating a third amenity for Londoners from the construction of the embankment. In the process Bazalgette left London with a strange anomaly. The Strand is so called because it used to run close to the river, the houses on the southern side backing on to the Thames so that their owners could step from into boats through York Gate and similar embarkation points. The creation of the Victoria Embankment has rearranged the geography of this part of London. The Strand, and York Gate, are now a considerable distance from the river but the names remain.

There was a fourth benefit which arose from the Victoria Embankment. Traffic congestion in London continued to mount and in the 1860s relief had been sought in the construction of the Metropolitan Railway, the world's first underground railway, which ran from Paddington to Farringdon in the City. The success of the

Like Shylock he [Gladstone] was entitled to his pound of flesh and he clutched it'.

York Gate; formerly an embarkation point for boats on the Thames now firmly on dry land in Victoria Embankment Gardens following Bazalgette's great works.

This artists's impression of the Victoria Embankment, near Charing Cross, was published in the Illustrated London News in June 1867. It shows the roadway being built above the low level sewer (2); a channel for service pipes (1); and the underground railway, now the District and Circle Line. A pneumatic railway (4) beneath the Thames was never built. No other metropolitan engineering project has ever solved so many problems at once. (By courtesy of the Guildhall Library, Corporation of London)

enterprise led to a desire to form a circular railway (the present Circle Line) which would encompass the central area of the City and Westminster. This required the construction of a line on the north bank of the river and Bazalgette constructed the embankment so that it would accommodate the line from Blackfriars to Westminster underground stations via Temple. Finally, with remarkable foresight, Bazalgette included in the embankment a small service tunnel to carry water, gas and, later, electricity ducts along the embankment, thus adding the fifth amenity to those already mentioned: the sewer, the much-needed road, the railway and the gardens. Appropriately, the

Victoria Embankment was the first part of London to be illuminated by electric light. A generator was installed close to the present site of Embankment underground station and eventually the whole length was lit by electric lights from Westminster to Blackfriars. The new lighting was an object of great curiosity, attracting crowds of sightseers after nightfall. The experiment continued until 1884 when the Jablochkoff company which provided the equipment went bankrupt and the area reverted to gas lights, but Londoners had seen the future.

Rarely can one civil engineering work have solved so many problems at one stroke

Rarely can one civil engineering work have solved so many problems at one stroke. Following its opening in July 1870 *The Times* summed up the feelings of Londoners when it wrote of the Victoria Embankment: 'For the principal engineer, of course, it will be a monument of enduring fame, second to none of the great achievements that have marked the Victorian Age'. In a just world Embankment underground station would be called Bazalgette station, but Sir Joseph has to be content with a smaller monument set into the embankment wall at the foot of Northumberland Avenue. One of the most remarkable features of the Victoria Embankment is that few people realise that it had to be built. A judge who sits in the High Court told the present author that he has occupied chambers overlooking the Embankment for over 30 years and had assumed that it had always been there, not realising the massive reclamation effort needed to create it. That admission is a tribute to its design. Few

St Thomas' Hospital, on land reclaimed by Bazalgette from the Thames, with the New Palace of Westminster in the background. (By courtesy of the Guildhall Library, Corporation of London)

engineering works of such a scale look as if they belong so naturally to their surroundings.

The Chelsea Embankment and the Albert Embankment

Bazalgette built two other embankments, thereby reclaiming a further 15 acres from the river and thus adding 52 acres in all to London's surface. The first was the Albert Embankment, which was built to protect from flooding the low-lying area between Vauxhall Bridge and Westminster Bridge on the south bank of the river in Lambeth. Again, it provided a much-needed road to relieve the area's congested streets and the reclaimed land provided a home for two of London's most notable buildings. The first is St Thomas's Hospital, which was relocated from Southwark to Bazalgette's reclaimed land opposite the Houses of Parliament. The second is the remarkable MI6 building at Vauxhall Cross, home of James Bond's colleagues since 1994, which also stands on reclaimed land. The Albert Embankment was the first to be opened, in 1869. Finally the Chelsea Embankment was constructed to carry the low level sewer from Battersea Bridge to Chelsea Bridge and to provide another thoroughfare through the metropolis. Following the opening of this, the last of his embankments, in July 1874, Bazalgette was knighted.

Thoroughfares, houses and open spaces

Reference has already been made to the traffic problems that plagued Victorian London which were only partially alleviated by Bazalgette's embankments and the underground railways they accommodated. In the 1850s a Parliamentary Select Committee on Metropolitan Communications[14] recommended that the proposed underground railway should be built; that all tolls on roads and bridges should be abolished; that new metropolitan thoroughfares should be constructed; and that Bazalgette's employers, the Metropolitan Board of Works, should bear the main responsibility for carrying out these improvements. These tasks were duly delegated to Bazalgette. In 1859 he presented to the Board a comprehensive plan which ran into difficulties from three quarters. First, each scheme for road improvements had to be submitted to the Home Secretary for his approval. Apart from the delay which this caused, the Home Secretary often exercised his power to forbid the demolition of slum dwellings until the Board had first rehoused them nearby. Given the shortage of affordable land this led to further delay. The second problem arose from the fact that the

'For the principal engineer, of course, it will be a monument of enduring fame, second to none of the great achievements that have marked the Victorian Age'.

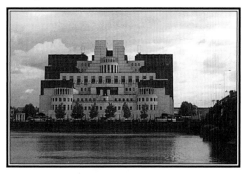

Vauxhall Cross, on land reclaimed by Bazalgette from the Thames.

Board had no powers of compulsory purchase so, having secured the Home Secretary's approval, the Board then had to embark upon tortuous negotiations with owners of property along the route. This often required the appointment of an arbitrator. The Board's Annual Report for 1860–1 described the process that had been necessary to create Garrick Street, Covent Garden. To build this street, 140 yards long, the Board had had to negotiate with 88 separate claimants with leasehold, freehold or trade interests. Their original claims for compensation amounted to £164,887, but after negotiation this figure was reduced to £97,687. The third problem arose from the fact that, though the money for these street improvements was raised from the ratepayers of London as a whole, the streets themselves were concentrated in a relatively small number of parishes in the central area. Representatives of other parishes, being a majority, could sometimes hold up schemes which did not benefit their area. The City Corporation, under the Lord Mayor, continued to enjoy a good deal of independence within the Square Mile of the City itself. It encouraged schemes which benefited the City and opposed those which didn't. In 1872 Bazalgette referred to:

> *'evidence of strong prejudice in favour of all street improvements within, or leading directly towards, the City and an equally strong objection to any which do not appear to lead the traffic direct into the City'.*[15]

Some street improvements presented problems of a diplomatic as well as a financial character. As construction of the Victoria Embankment proceeded it became clear that it would be necessary to provide better access to this new thoroughfare from the direction of Trafalgar Square. A major obstacle lay in the form of Northumberland House, the palatial London home of the Duke of Northumberland, which lay on the south side of the square with extensive gardens stretching towards the river. In 1866 the Board approached the Duke and offered to purchase it but the Duke, who had only succeeded to the title the previous year, answered that he wanted to enjoy the inheritance for which he had waited so long. The Board could have asked the Home Secretary to intervene, but the Duke was a popular figure in the House of Lords. His cause was further helped by sentiment, since his was the last of the great houses which, from mediaeval times, had occupied the southern side of the Strand, stretching from John of Gaunt's Savoy Palace to Trafalgar Square. In 1873, following the death of the Duke, the Board approached his successor, who took a more cavalier and commercial attitude to the

To build this street, 140 yards long, the Board had had to negotiate with 88 separate claimants

fate of his ancestral home and gladly sold it for the colossal sum of £500,000. Bazalgette set to work immediately and Northumberland Avenue opened in 1876.

St Martin-in-the-Fields

Problems of a different kind were encountered when Bazalgette proposed building Charing Cross Road. First, he had to demolish the notorious St Giles tenements, some of the worst slums in London, south of the present Tottenham Court Road underground station. Initially, a medical officer declared the dwellings unfit for human use. Then the Board had to check the titles of the numerous tenants and property owners who could be relied upon to claim compensation. Next the Home Secretary appointed an arbitrator to adjudicate on the claims. This could be costly and time-consuming, not least because compensation could be awarded on the basis that the properties could be valued as 'going concerns' even though they had been condemned. Then the Board had to rehouse the tenants before it could demolish the slums. The situation was eased when new legislation awarded compensation on an 'unfit for use' basis and the Board was also permitted to resell land for commercial use and rehouse tenants elsewhere provided that they could travel to work on workmen's trains, the fares limited to a penny a mile.

Despite these helpful measures it took six years to construct Charing Cross Road and Bazalgette had one final obstacle to overcome: the church of St Martin-in-the-Fields. James Gibbs's masterpiece had been consecrated in 1726 but it now stood in the path of Charing Cross Road as it made its slow but relentless way towards Trafalgar Square. Bazalgette proposed, rather insensitively, to slice though the steps that adorn the church's fine classical portico and brick up the portico itself. It is hard to disagree with the parishioners' petition which complained that 'with the steps removed, and the front walled up, the portico would appear unmeaning, and would be an architectural monstrosity'. The petitioners had made their point. Bazalgette re-aligned the road and the great church was spared.[16]

Bazalgette made many other additions to London's streets. In its final report the Board was able to describe 42 major improvements to London's thoroughfares. In addition to those already mentioned they included Shaftesbury Avenue, Queen Victoria Street, Theobalds Road, Southwark Street and Great Eastern Street. In the process he demolished 7,403 tenements, mostly slums, and rehoused 38,231 people.[17]

River crossings

The Board turned its attention to the abolition of tolls on bridges

'with the steps removed, and the front walled up, the portico would appear unmeaning, and would be an architectural monstrosity'

across the Thames in 1876. Prior to this time the only toll-free bridges within the metropolis were London, Blackfriars, Southwark and Westminster bridges. The other bridges usually charged a halfpenny for a pedestrian to cross and threepence for a carriage. A Parliamentary Committee estimated that a labourer living in the cheaper areas south of the river would pay tolls of 24 shillings a year out of an annual wage of £40 to £50. The Metropolitan Toll Bridges Bill, introduced in 1876, enabled the Board to buy out the owners of the bridges and free them of tolls. The Act had some annoying consequences. Waterloo Bridge, built by John Rennie in 1817, had never made any money for its shareholders since travellers made the short detour to the toll-free Westminster or Blackfriars bridges. When the Board introduced its Bill to Parliament the value of Waterloo Bridge shares rose from £2 to £12 (though they had originally cost the unfortunate shareholders £100).[18] It didn't do them any good. After the Bill became an Act in 1877 Bazalgette surveyed the bridge and his experienced eye revealed that it was in a very poor condition. The bridge, which had cost £1,054,000 to build in 1817, was bought by the Board for £474,200 and Bazalgette immediately spent a further £62,705 on strengthening its foundations. The freeing of the bridge from tolls occurred at midday on Saturday 5 October 1878 and was reported as a great occasion. As the hour approached pedestrians jostled one another in an attempt to be the last to pay the halfpenny toll. The toll-keepers, wearing their white aprons with huge pockets, finally stood aside, guns were fired in salute from the Surrey shore and crowds surged across the bridge.[19]

guns were fired in salute from the Surrey shore and crowds surged across the bridge.

In May 1879, a more elaborate ceremony marked the freeing of the Lambeth, Chelsea, Battersea, Vauxhall and Albert bridges. The Prince and Princess of Wales declared the bridges toll-free and then drove across each in turn. Chelsea pensioners paraded in their uniforms, guns fired in salute, flotillas of boats were bedecked with flags, children sang 'God Bless the Prince of Wales' and the four-mile route was lined with cheering crowds.[20] A year later a similar ceremony freed Putney, Wandsworth and Hammersmith bridges. Bazalgette's surveys revealed that most of them required only minor repairs to accommodate the extra traffic generated by the abolition of tolls but there were exceptions. Hammersmith Bridge had been opened in 1827 as the first suspension bridge across the Thames but it was too weak and too narrow to handle the additional traffic that now used it. When Bazalgette's inspection revealed that bits of it had started to fall off he closed, widened and substantially reconstructed it. It carried an ever-increasing burden of traffic, including heavy goods vehicles and double-decker buses which were beyond Bazalgette's imagination, until 1994, when it was temporarily closed for repairs. At the same time the nearby Hammersmith flyover, built a century later, was also closed for repairs. Hammersmith Bridge also survived two attempts by the IRA to blow it up. Bazalgette built his structures to last.

The bridges at Battersea and Putney were beyond repair. The wooden bridge at Battersea, built by Earl Spencer in 1772, was demolished and replaced by Bazalgette's five-arch span design in wrought iron, opened in 1890. A wooden bridge at Putney had been erected in 1729 by a company whose shareholders included the then Prime Minister, Robert Walpole. By 1880 it had become decrepit so it was demolished and replaced by Bazalgette's handsome granite structure. The new approaches to the bridge from the north, which Bazalgette added to accommodate the growing volume of traffic, prompted the landlord of the Eight Bells public house, Fulham, to sue the Board for loss of trade on the grounds that his premises had been bypassed. He was awarded compensation of £1,000.

New crossings

When Bazalgette took office in 1856 the lowest bridge on the Thames was London Bridge, yet one third of the inhabitants of the metropolis lived below this point and had no other means of crossing the river on foot. Bazalgette prepared three plans for crossings downstream. First he proposed a bridge between the Tower of London and St Olave's parish on the south bank. He suggested a bridge with long approach roads which would enable pedestrians and horse-drawn vehicles to cross the river at sufficient height to enable shipping to pass beneath the bridge through the Pool of London. The City of London Corporation's response was lukewarm. They responded that 'the need for any bridge or tunnel did not seem sufficiently proved to justify the Corporation taking part in the promotion of such a scheme.' On the opposite bank the vestrymen of St Olave's viewed with alarm the prospect of eastenders using the bridge to mount an invasion of their parish, complaining that the bridge would 'have a prejudicial effect on the value of a large amount of property in the parish'.[21] Nevertheless the authorities pressed ahead. Bazalgette's design was rejected in favour of the famous bascule design which, in 1894, opened as Tower Bridge.

Bazalgette also proposed a crossing further downstream in the form of a tunnel at Blackwall. One of his last acts before retirement was to let the contracts for its construction. Finally, he proposed the institution of a free ferry at Woolwich. The necessary works were undertaken under his direction and the service began shortly after the Metropolitan Board handed over its responsibilities to the new London County Council in January, 1889, and Bazalgette retired.

the bridge would 'have a prejudicial effect on the value of a large amount of property in the parish'.

Parks and open spaces

The Metropolitan Board's responsibilities included the creation of parks and other open spaces at a time when the fresh air they offered the inhabitants of crowded tenements was the only medicine that many doctors could offer. Florence Nightingale was a particularly ardent advocate of the benefits of fresh air in her *Notes on Nursing*. The many parks which Bazalgette was responsible for laying out and landscaping include Battersea Park, Kennington Park, Victoria Park, Hackney Park and Clissold Park, Stoke Newington. The 63-acre Southwark Park was opened in 1869 after Bazalgette had spent £99,740 clearing and landscaping the site and in the same year the 115-acre Finsbury Park opened at a cost of £111,000. By the time the Board left office in 1889 it was managing 2,603 acres of public parks.

Leicester Square: a strange benefactor

One of the stranger episodes in the career of Bazalgette brought him into contact with one of Queen Victoria's more exotic subjects. It concerned the refurbishment of Leicester Square. The area took its name from Leicester House, the London home of the earls of Leicester, which had been built in 1636. The future George II, while Prince of Wales, had resided there in the 18th century and used it as a base from which to pursue his endless quarrels with his father, George I. Later in the century it became the home of George II's son Frederick, Prince of Wales, who continued the Hanoverian tradition of pursuing a vendetta against his father. In 1737, as an additional irritant to his father, Frederick unveiled an equestrian statue of his grandfather, George I. In 1806 Leicester House was demolished and the square became derelict. Various enterprises devoted to public entertainment arose in the square, the most memorable being the 'Royal Panopticon of Science and Art' which was opened in 1854 'to exhibit and illustrate, in a popular form, discoveries in science and art'. It failed and was sold in 1857 to a theatrical impresario who sold the Panopticon's organ to St Paul's Cathedral and re-opened it the following year as the Alhambra Palace theatre. In this form it survived until 1936 as a venue for such entertainments as circuses, gymnastic performances by the Frenchman Léotard and Diaghilev's Ballet Russe. In the meantime the rest of the square was becoming derelict. In the 1780s one side of the square had been damaged in the anti-Catholic Gordon riots and in 1865 a gas explosion reduced the buildings on the same side of the square to rubble, the explosion causing such a sensation that the Prince of Wales (later Edward VII) arrived on the scene and was given a conducted tour of the wreckage wearing a fireman's helmet. In the meantime the equestrian statue was being

Various enterprises devoted to public entertainment arose in the square

systematically vandalised, horse and rider being gradually deprived of legs and arms respectively. It succumbed to its final indignity on the night of 16/17 October 1866. The chief suspects were the staff of the nearby Alhambra Theatre, since theatrical props were used to paint white blotches on the horse, which was also bedecked with horns. The rider was equipped with a dunce's cap and a sweep's brush.[22]

By this time the Metropolitan Board of Works was becoming increasingly embarrassed by the condition of the square and entered into long and acrimonious negotiations with the principal freeholder of the surrounding properties, a wine merchant called James Tulk. Tulk, in an attempt to raise the stakes, sold the equestrian statue for scrap and allowed an advertising agent to erect an ugly hoarding, 12 feet high, around the square, on which were advertised 'cocoa, cheap trousers, rival circuses and the largest circulation [newspapers]'. Writs flew and the Metropolitan Board deposited a Bill in Parliament which would have enabled it to acquire the square regardless of Tulk's wishes. A Leicester Square Defence Committee was formed by angry residents who began a lawsuit in the court of Chancery.

The mysterious baron: Albert Grant *né* Gottheimer

Albert Grant now appeared as a *deus ex machina*. He had been born in Dublin in 1831 as Abraham Gottheimer. He established himself in the City of London as a 'company promoter' and may be regarded as an early exponent of the black art of direct mailing. He obtained the names and addresses of 'clergy, widows and other small but sanguine investors ... greedy to take up companies quicker than he could bring them out' and sent to them prospectuses of companies with enticing names and even more enticing promises of profits beyond the dreams of avarice: the Emma Silver Mine; the Odessa Waterworks; the Labuan Coal Company and the Imperial Bank of China were among them. Nearly all of these enterprises led to lawsuits and of £24,000,000 raised from hopeful subscribers £20,000,000 was lost. Grant made his money from commissions. In 1865 he had been elected as MP for Kidderminster but was unseated following allegations of bribery. In 1868 Victor Emmanuel I created him a hereditary baron of the newly created kingdom of Italy for financial assistance to the city of Milan and thereafter he styled himself Baron Grant.[23]

In January 1874, this unlikely benefactor informed the Metropolitan Board of Works that he had acquired James Tulk's interest in Leicester Square and was in the process of acquiring the remaining freeholds. His task had been made easier by the case in Chancery, which was moving against James Tulk's interests. 'Baron'

theatrical props were used to paint white blotches on the horse, which was also bedecked with horns

an early exponent of the black art of direct mailing

Grant informed the Board that he proposed to clean up the square and lay it out as a garden decorated with statues of former residents which eventually included busts of Isaac Newton, Joshua Reynolds, William Hogarth and the surgeon John Hunter. He would then hand it over to the Board. A no doubt wary Board, and its Chief Engineer, proceeded to negotiate with Grant, wisely refraining from asking where the money was coming from for this grand gesture. Grant was later declared bankrupt and died in penury in 1899.

The ceremony in which Grant handed over the square on 2 July 1874, was afforded generous coverage in London newspapers. *The Times* informed its readers that 'Mr Grant's speech, if not very short, was almost all to the purpose'.[24] The square remains the central feature of London's theatre district, a statue of Charlie Chaplin having been more recently added to those bequeathed by Albert Grant. The central statue, that of Shakespeare, carries an inscription which reminds passers-by of Grant's generous gesture, albeit one made with other people's money.

'Mr Grant's speech, if not very short, was almost all to the purpose'

Bazalgette's legacy

Bazalgette's memory, however, does not depend upon his brief association with Albert Grant. The streets, parks and bridges that he created changed the face of London for ever. The main drainage and the associated embankments were the largest civil engineering enterprise of the 19th century, perhaps the largest ever, carried out under the supervision of one man. At times this project alone was employing 20,000 people. His achievement is perhaps best summed up in the words of *The Times* obituary which appeared on Monday 16 March 1891, the day after his death:

> *'When the New Zealander comes to London, a thousand years hence, to sketch the ruins of St Paul's, the magnificent solidity and the faultless symmetry of the great granite blocks which form the wall of the Thames Embankment will still remain to testify that, in the reign of Victoria, 'jerry-building' was not quite universal. Of the great sewer that runs beneath Londoners know, as a rule, nothing though the Registrar-General could tell them that its existence has added some twenty years to their chance of life'.*

[1] Doxat, J. *The Living Thames, the Restoration of a Great Tidal River*, Hutchinson Benham, 1977.

[2] This information is extracted from papers in the Royal Archives which are quoted with the gracious permission of Her Majesty the Queen; also from Jean Louis' accounts in the archives of Coutts Bank.

[3] Chadwick, E. *Report on the Sanitary Condition of the Labouring Population of Great Britain*, Edinburgh University Press edition, 1965, page 117.

[4] *The Times*, 9 July 1855.

[5] See Chapter 5 above for a discussion of the issue of Big Ben's name.

[6] *Hansard*, 3rd series, vol.150, 11 June 1858.

[7] Metropolitan Board of Works, Document 2431/1, clause 45; available in the Metropolitan Archives.

[8] *The Observer*, 14 April 1861; the later quotation is taken from *The Observer*, 6 July 1862.

[9] Metropolitan Board of Works *Minutes*, 28 April 1865.

[10] Metropolitan Board of Works, Miscellaneous Reports, No.23, *The Extraordinary Rainfall on Friday, 26th July, 1867.*

[11] The *Illustrated London News*, 10, 17 and 24 September 1892, chronicled the epidemic in Hamburg and the anxiety it engendered in London.

[12] *Cassell's Saturday Journal*, 30 August 1890, page 1160.

[13] *The Times*, 11 July 1870; 12 months later, on 14 July 1871, the newspaper celebrated W.H. Smith's victory over Gladstone's Government.

[14] Parliamentary papers, 1854–5, vol.10, contains the committee's deliberations.

[15] Bazalgette's report on the matter is held in the British Library catalogue No.8229.99.30.

[16] Metropolitan Board of Works *Minutes of Proceedings*, 24 November 1876.

[17] Metropolitan Board of Works *Annual Report*, 1888, page 146 records the programme of improvements to dwellings.

[18] Parliamentary papers, 1877, vol.14; the committee gave the company chairman, William Clarke, a hard time on the matter of the share price.

[19] The *Daily Chronicle*, 7 October 1878, described the occasion.

[20] The *Illustrated London News* described this occasion, with illustrations, on 31 May 1879.

[21] Metropolitan Board of Works, *Minutes of Proceedings*, 22 March 1878, records the objections.

[22] Taylor, T. *Leicester Square*, Bickers, London, 1874; and Hollingshead, J., *The Story of Leicester Square*, Simpkin Marshall, London, 1892, give an account of the condition into which the square had fallen.

[23] The *Dictionary of Business Biography*, Butterworths, 1984, vol.2 has an account of Grant's career.

[24] *The Times*, 3 July 1874.

CHAPTER 7

Sir Edward Watkin, the Metropolitan Railway and Metroland

Sir Edward Watkin.
(London's Transport
Museum)

*'out of the mist arose
Sir Edward Watkin's dream
An Eiffel Tower for London'*
(Sir John Betjeman in *Metroland*, BBC2,
1973)

*'The actual practical working of a railway
was a subject he had never
studied and never really understood'.*
(Sir Edward Watkin's obituary, in *The
Times*, 15 April 1901)

SIR Edward Watkin (1819–1901) was a force of nature. Born the son of a moderately prosperous cotton merchant in the reign of George III, by the time of his death in the 20th century he had founded a newspaper, chaired three railway companies, been an MP for three constituencies, begun to dig a Channel tunnel and failed to build a superior version of the Eiffel Tower on a site which later became world-famous for other reasons. He had been knighted for his services in helping to give Canada an effective rail network. He had also taken the first steps in the creation of 'Metroland', the very symbol of middle-class suburban London celebrated in the poetry of John

Betjeman. From this incomplete list of his achievements it would be reasonable to conclude that he was a busy man. In fact he could fairly be described as a nervous and aggressive workaholic who from his twenties onwards suffered from anxiety, depression and nervous breakdown. He could be a very difficult man to work with. He conducted a long-running feud with a rival railway chairman who would have been useful as an ally and could be appallingly rude to shareholders at annual general meetings of the companies he chaired. He refused to have any dealings with trade unions but saw to it that the clerks of his companies were given a turkey, a goose or a leg of mutton at Christmas. He was the best-known railwayman of the later 19th century despite the fact that he never chaired any of the great companies like the LNER or the Great Western. He was also an enigma.

A Manchester free trader

Edward Watkin was born in Salford in 1819, the same year as Joseph Bazalgette. His father, Absalom, was a prosperous Manchester cotton merchant. George III's long reign was drawing to its close and only 11 years would pass before the opening of the railway from Liverpool to Watkin's native Manchester. He joined his father's business when he was about 15 but does not appear to have been a particularly dedicated employee, since by the time he was 20 he was heavily engaged in local politics. At that age he was a sufficiently committed free trader to have become secretary of a local anti-Corn Law association, the aim of which was to remove the protective duties on grain that increased the price of bread and offended the principles of free trade. In 1845, aged 26, he founded the *Manchester Examiner* to support this cause. In 1840, aged 21, he had been recruited to the ranks of the Manchester Athenaeum, a learned society which was flirting with insolvency, and he restored its finances by persuading Charles Dickens and Benjamin Disraeli to conduct soirées on its premises. Such energy was later to be applied to rescuing insolvent railways. He also campaigned successfully for a Saturday half-holiday for Manchester clerks and raised money for the purchase of three local parks.

The railwayman

His railway career began in 1845 when he became secretary to the small Trent Valley Railway Company. In 1853 he became general manager of the Manchester, Sheffield and Lincolnshire Railway Company, with which he remained associated for the next 41 years, the last 30 as chairman. This rather unusual railway resulted from the

He conducted a long-running feud with a rival railway chairman who would have been useful as an ally and could be appallingly rude to shareholders at annual general meetings

he restored its finances by persuading Charles Dickens and Benjamin Disraeli to conduct soirées on its premises

earlier merger of a number of smaller lines and linked Grimsby on the east coast with Liverpool and Chester in the west via Sheffield and Manchester. It became the vehicle of Watkin's ambition to link Manchester first with London and then with Paris via a Channel tunnel. He hoped thereby to make himself the greatest railway magnate of the age, but this ambition ensured that, under his chairmanship, the railway expanded rather than flourished, dividends remaining consistently low. He berated other railway chairmen for failing to aid him in achieving this ambition, criticising the august Lord Colville of the Great Northern for 'wasting your shareholders' capital on the plastering of your old line' when he could have joined with Watkin in creating a new one. The first steps towards Paris were taken in the 1890s and involved the construction of the 'London Extension' from Annesley, north of Nottingham, via Leicester to Quainton, near Aylesbury in Buckinghamshire. Quainton was the northern extremity of the Metropolitan Railway, of which Watkin had become chairman in 1872.

He berated other railway chairmen for failing to aid him

The politician

In the meantime Edward Watkin had built a successful political career. He was briefly elected as MP for Yarmouth in 1857 but was unseated following allegations that his money had been used to buy votes, a common feature of parliamentary elections before secret ballots were introduced in 1872. Watkin himself was probably not directly involved in the bribery and the setback did not prevent him from being returned as a Liberal for two other constituencies: Stockport in 1864–8 and Folkestone and Hythe, where he sat between 1874 and 1895. In 1868 he was one of 78 MPs who voted unsuccessfully to give the vote to women in the 1868 Reform Bill. In 1861, at the request of the Government, he spent some time in Canada advising on the creation of a national railway network and it was for this contribution to the process of uniting that vast dominion that he was knighted in 1868 and created a baronet in 1880.

The Metropolitan

When Sir Edward Watkin became chairman of the Metropolitan in 1872 the railway was in a sorry state. It had opened on 9 January 1863, the world's first underground railway, to link the Great Western Railway's terminus at Paddington to Farringdon, in the City of London, via Euston and King's Cross. It was operated by steam engines which were fitted with special condensers to minimise the escape of steam and smoke into the enclosed tunnels, a device which enjoyed only partial success. By 1872 it had been extended to South

Kensington in the west and Moorgate in the south. This was an early attempt to alleviate the chronic congestion on London's streets, which was celebrated in the work of the artist Gustave Doré. For most of its length the Metropolitan ran just below street level along the line of the Marylebone Road, Euston Road, Pentonville Road and City Road, before turning south to the City beneath the Farringdon Road. In some places, as at Farringdon, it runs in an open cutting. Despite the relatively simple 'cut and cover' methods used to construct the line, the cost of building a railway beneath the streets of the world's largest Metropolis was then, as now, very high. The difficulties that had been encountered in financing its construction were a portent of the problems that were to beset underground railways for the next century and a half. An attempt to build the much-needed line in the 1850s was frustrated when £170,000 which had been set aside by the Great Northern railway to buy shares in the project was embezzled by one of its officers. The culprit, Leopold Redpath, was one of the last convicts to be transported to Australia for his misdeeds but his conduct was symptomatic of the problems and chicanery that came to characterize the financing of London's underground railways. In 1904 Whitaker Wright, promoter of the Bakerloo Line, committed suicide after being sentenced to seven years hard labour for fraud in connection with the project. The following year the American

The culprit, Leopold Redpath, was one of the last convicts to be transported to Australia for his misdeeds

CHARLES TYSON YERKES (1837–1905)

Charles Tyson Yerkes was born in Philadelphia in 1837 where he set himself up as a banker and stockbroker, selling municipal bonds to his fellow citizens. The unorthodox nature of his methods led to a spell in gaol after which he moved to Chicago. There, his declared motto 'buy up old junk, fix it up a little and unload it upon other fellows' was applied to that city's municipal transport and led to a gathering of defrauded investors outside city hall brandishing nooses and firearms. In 1901 he came to London and, by a series of intricate financial manoeuvres, acquired controlling interests in four underground railways; the ailing District; the half-completed Bakerloo; the unbuilt Piccadilly; and the unbuilt Charing Cross, Euston and Hampstead Railway – the northern half of what later became the Northern Line. He also began the process of electrifying the Inner Circle. At his death in December 1905 he left his empire on the brink of ruin, from which it was rescued by the German-born banker Sir Edgar Speyer. Upon such men as Yerkes did early 20th century Londoners depend for their urban transport.

financier Charles Tyson Yerkes died in New York leaving his lines, the District, Piccadilly, Bakerloo and Northern,[1] on the brink of bankruptcy.

In comparison with these fiascos the Metropolitan was at least respectable, but its dividends were poor. This unhappy situation arose from the fact that competition for passengers from horse-drawn (and later motorised) buses in the center of the metropolis kept fares to levels which made it hard to generate the profits required to pay acceptable dividends on the capital invested in constructing the line. This did not, however, deter other entrepreneurs from building other underground railways. The Metropolitan District railway (later the District Line) had been launched in 1854 to create the southern half of what would eventually become the Circle Line. By the time Watkin took over as chairman of the Metropolitan in 1872 the District was running from High Street Kensington, where its services overlapped those of the Metropolitan, to Mansion House, within half a mile of the metropolitan terminus at Moorgate. It took more than a decade of quarrelling between the chairmen of the two companies before the circle was closed.

In 1872, as he took up the post of chairman of the Metropolitan, Watkin faced problems more pressing than his relations with the District. He first had to restore the ailing finances of the Metropolitan to a condition in which a reasonable dividend could be paid to its long-suffering shareholders, whose rebellion had led to his appointment. He set about this task by the time-honoured device of abusing and deriding his predecessors. An audit of the company's affairs revealed a sorry tale. The company's accounts were in such a state of confusion that it was far from clear what profits, if any, the line was making. Many 'false and fictitious entries' were discovered in the stores inventory and the chief engineer resigned when his department's expenditure was shown to be out of control.[2] Watkin appointed Edwin Waterhouse, founding partner of accountants Price Waterhouse,[3] to undertake a further investigation to 'ascertain what the defects in the past management may have been which have brought the company to such a low ebb'.

This brief could be seen as pre-judging the outcome of Waterhouse's enquiry, but the eminent accountant had no difficulty providing Watkin with the evidence he sought. His report revealed that Watkin's predecessor as chairman, a man named Parson, had admitted that he didn't understand the accounts. The stores had been 'grossly mismanaged' and the stores manager had vanished with the rewards of his mismanagement. Extravagant sums had been paid to engineers, notably an engineer called John Fowler, who had been

the time-honoured device of abusing and deriding his predecessors

involved in the affairs of the Metropolitan and the District companies from their earliest days. The modest dividends that had been paid had been drawn from capital.

Watkin now set about reordering the affairs of the company in the combative style that was to become his hallmark. He appointed a competent accountant and purged the board of most of the members installed by the wretched Parson. Watkin's salary was doubled. He then turned his wrath on John Fowler, reminding him that he had claimed almost half a million pounds from the Metropolitan and District railways. Referring to this unimaginably large sum, half a *billion* in 21st century terms, Watkin opened his letter to Fowler with the engaging assurance that he had no wish to quarrel and wrote:[4]

> *'no engineer in the world was ever so highly paid ... you have set an example which seems to me to have largely aided in the de-moralisation of the Professional men of all sorts who have lived upon the suffering shareholders for the past ten years'.*

He concluded by adding 'I apologise in advance if I have given any offence'. Later in the year, in a speech to shareholders, he returned to the theme with a reference to 'Clodd, the great railway contractor, Plausible the great railway engineer and Vampire, the great railway lawyer'. His relentless pursuit of enemies of the Metropolitan continued throughout his chairmanship. In 1889 he turned his scorn on an obscure soldier called Sir Randall Roberts, who had sued the railway for an injury supposedly incurred on the company's premises, claiming £5,000. Watkin had him followed by a private detective whose evidence as to the negligible effect of Roberts's supposed injuries resulted in the award of damages of £10 – a fraction of his costs.

'I apologise in advance if I have given any offence'

Closing the circle

Watkin now turned his attention to more constructive activities: linking up with the District to create the Circle Line and extending the Metropolitan in a north-westerly direction to create the suburbs that were to become known as Metroland. The first task was to close the gap between the District station at Mansion House and the Metropolitan at Moorgate in order to create the Circle Line linking the main line termini north of the Thames. This process was not helped by Watkin's long-running feud with the chairman of the District Railway, James Staats Forbes (1823–1904).

Forbes was what would now be called a company doctor who, besides being chairman of the District, also headed the London, Chatham and Dover Railway. Neither railway had proved a good investment for its shareholders. The District was permanently short of funds and the London, Chatham and Dover was rescued from the brink of insolvency by Forbes when he became its chairman in 1861. In both capacities he came into contact, and more often conflict, with Watkin. The latter was by this time chairman of the East London Railway which ran from Whitechapel to New Cross; and of the South-Eastern Railway which ran from London to Dover and was thus a competitor to Forbes's London, Chatham and Dover line. Watkin considered that the public interest would be served if the two main line railways were merged, under his chairmanship of course, but Forbes resisted this until 1899, five years after Watkin's retirement. In the meantime Watkin had to content himself with drawing comparisons between the fortunes of the two lines, to the advantage of his own.

he came into contact, and more often conflict, with Watkin

He was even more ruthless in his criticism of the District. At this time the payment of a dividend on the ordinary shares of the District was a very rare event owing to the levels of debt which the line had incurred during its construction. In January 1890 Watkin entertained his laughing shareholders by reminding them of the fate of the holders of District shares and contrasting their wretched lot with the good fortune of the Metropolitan shares since he, Sir Edward Watkin, had been chairman. This went down well at annual general meetings but it was no way to gain the support of Forbes, who would have been a useful ally and who commented that more friends were won by sugar than by vinegar. In the meantime the completion of the Circle Line was dependent upon a suspension of the feud between the two men.

more friends were won by sugar than by vinegar

Peace breaks out

In December 1877 Charles Lucas, a contractor, persuaded Forbes and Watkin to hold a meeting in the neutral surroundings of his office in the City. The City agreed to contribute £300,000 to the cost of completing the Circle and the Metropolitan Board of Works eventually agreed to contribute £500,000.[5] It was agreed that the two railways would extend their lines to a meeting point at Tower Hill. In September 1881 the work began, following some characteristically combative interventions and threats from Watkin. Thus, in January of that year he wrote to the secretary of the City Sewers Commission protesting about a meeting a few weeks earlier about the rail link: 'Having noticed the insulting tone of the discussion I am beginning to think that the whole scheme must be abandoned'.[6] The Metropolitan reached Tower Hill in September 1882 and had to wait two years for the financially strained District to complete the link.

The resumption of hostilities

Trial working of trains around the system began in October, with a full service beginning on 6 October 1884. It was agreed that Metropolitan trains would run clockwise around the outer track while District trains ran anti-clockwise on the inner. It was anticipated that this would avoid conflicts between the two companies but the hope was vain. Forbes and Watkin blamed each other for running more than their fair share of trains, causing delays at crossing points. An argument flared over the right to park locomotives at a certain siding at South Kensington station.

The District left locomotives there. The Metropolitan removed them. The District retaliated by fastening its engine to the buffers with chains. The Metropolitan sent one, two and finally three of its locomotives to remove the offending object. In the words of the *West London Advertiser* 'a tug-of-war ensued in which the chained train came off the victor'.

For passengers other problems were more pressing. Trains were running up to three hours late and one group of desperate passengers staged a breakout from a train marooned between stations. In October 1881, two weeks after the line opened, an arbitrator was appointed to examine the grievances of the two companies. Watkin asked him to 'put us out of our misery'. This brave man suggested that each company should restrict itself to eight trains an hour, allowing 80 minutes to complete the circle. The truce would last three months before the situation was reviewed. The insults, however, continued. Watkin told his shareholders that the treacherous District had sneaked in an extra 46 trains a day, thus causing difficulties 'shamefully and needlessly made'. The word 'shamefully' has been deleted in the official records by a scribe more sensitive than Watkin but is clearly evident to the careful reader.[7] Each company at this time had its own booking office at each station on the Circle and Forbes retaliated by claiming that the Metropolitan was cheating passengers by sending them the long way round the Circle when this resulted in more revenue for Watkin's company. He also informed his long-suffering shareholders that yet again no dividend would be paid. Questioned on the possibility of a merger between the two companies Watkin dismissed the idea on the grounds of the District's unprofitability while Forbes told his shareholders that 'the time for celebrating the wedding would arrive when the chairman of the Metropolitan company entertained different views from those which he had recently

'a tug-of-war ensued in which the chained train came off the victor'

the Metropolitan was cheating passengers by sending them the long way round the Circle

expressed regarding the condition and prospects of the Metropolitan District company'.[8]

'These Underground railways must soon be discontinued'

The work of completing the circle had been made more expensive by the attempt of the Metropolitan Board of Works to eliminate the ventilation shafts ('blow holes') in the streets, through which smoke and steam could escape from the tunnels into the atmosphere. Even with the shafts in place the atmosphere in the tunnels was appalling. The specially designed 'condensing engines' were only partially successful in reducing the volume of steam emitted by the locomotives and did nothing to eliminate the smoke which came from their chimneys. A letter to *The Times* described the situation on the Metropolitan Railway in 1879:[9]

> *'I was almost suffocated and was obliged to be assisted from the train at an intermediate station. On reaching the open air I requested to be taken to a chemist close at hand. Without a moment's hesitation he said 'Oh, I see, Metropolitan Railway', and at once poured out a wine glass of what I conclude he designated Metropolitan Mixture. I was induced to ask him whether he often had such cases, to which he rejoined 'Why, bless you Sir, we often have twenty cases a day'.*

The situation on the Circle line was much worse, with eight trains an hour in each direction and a smaller proportion of stations in open cuttings. An early journey on the Circle was described by the journalist R.D. Blumenfeld[10] as 'my first experience of Hades ... The atmosphere was a mixture of sulphur, coal dust and foul fumes from the gas lamps so that by the time we reached Moorgate I was near dead of asphyxiation ... I should think these Underground railways must soon be discontinued, for they are a menace to health'.

they wanted a direct current which would do away with an engine altogether

The solution to this problem was eventually to be found in electrification, but Watkin's grasp of the finer points of this novel form of traction was unsure. He was particularly confused by the distinction between direct current and alternating current. In 1889 when questioned by shareholders on the matter he explained that 'The proposal was to have a carriage containing electric motors but the Board had come to the conclusion that they wanted a direct current which would do away with an engine altogether'.[11] In 1898 a Board of Trade committee enquired into the state of the tunnels and was told that 550 passenger and goods trains were using the system each day, all drawn by steam engines. By this time Watkin had retired and his successors tried to persuade the committee that the foul air of the tunnels was beneficial to health. Colonel John Bell, the general manager of the Metropolitan, insisted that Great Portland Street station was 'actually used as a sanatorium for men who had been afflicted with asthma and bronchial complaints'.[12] The committee may have been less reassured by the testimony of a driver called Langford who, having told them of his excellent health following 34 years service in the fuming tunnels, added that 'very seldom' was the smoke so thick as to render the signals invisible! Electrification of the Circle would have to wait for the following century and the intervention of the American Charles Tyson Yerkes.[13]

'very seldom' was the smoke so thick as to render the signals invisible!

Manchester to Paris with Sir Edward Watkin

Sir Edward Watkin now turned his attention to his grandest project: a railway network running from Manchester to Paris under the control of himself. There were five components in this scheme. The first was the Manchester, Sheffield and Lincolnshire Railway which, via its 'London Extension', would link with the second, the Metropolitan, at Quainton Junction. The latter had been acquired when Watkin, on behalf of the Metropolitan, purchased the Aylesbury and Buckingham Railway in 1891, thus taking the Metropolitan to the rural wilderness of the Vale of Aylesbury. This move was not without its critics. One shareholder suggested at an annual meeting that the Aylesbury line was fit only for 'ducks and drakes and donkeys' and begged the directors to concentrate on the primary purpose of the railway, which was to carry passengers beneath the congested streets of the metropolis. This was a difficult argument to counter. A branch of the Aylesbury and Buckingham Railway ran from Quainton, itself an isolated community,

Quainton, Bucks, hub of Sir Edward Watkin's dream of a railway from Manchester to Paris.

Shunting operations were carried out by a horse

to the hilltop village of Brill. Even in 1963 this was so remote that the nearby Leatherslade Farm was chosen by the Great Train Robbers as a hideout after their audacious robbery. The carriages to Brill were drawn by a tiny chain-driven locomotive (now in London's Transport Museum) at a speed of 4mph. Shunting operations were carried out by a horse and when carriages came off the ill-maintained track farm labourers joined the passengers in pushing them back on to the rails. This was the home of Thomas the Tank Engine rather than the heart of the metropolis.[14]

Watkin was not to be diverted from his vision by such distractions. He justified his actions by claiming, with some justification, that longer-distance commuter traffic would be more profitable than the carriage of passengers within the metropolis in the face of competition from buses. In 1891 he told his shareholders of the advantages of the proposed link with his Manchester, Sheffield and Lincolnshire Railway at Quainton Road: 'The benefits to your undertaking generally would be very considerable and your Directors have entered into an agreement with the Sheffield company for running powers for that company over your system between Quainton Road and Baker Street'.[15] The last few miles into London for the main line railway aroused the opposition of the artistic community of St John's Wood, headed by the painter Alma-Tadema. Worse, it incurred the hostility of the Marylebone Cricket Club, which was appalled to learn that the

Chain locomotive used on the outer reaches of 'Metroland'. (London's Transport Museum)

London terminus was to be sited close to the hallowed turf at Lord's. Watkin was threatened with the wrath of W.G. Grace and the demon Australian bowler F.R. Spofforth. Peace was made with the MCC when the site of the London terminus was moved. The Manchester, Sheffield and Lincolnshire Railway was eventually transformed, after Watkin's retirement, into the Great Central Railway with its London terminus at Marylebone. This was the last of the London terminus stations to be opened, in 1899, and Watkin attended the event in a wheelchair. At Watkin's insistence the Great Central had been built to accommodate continental gauge trains, the only railway in Great Britain that could do so. The cost to shareholders of the 'London Extension' was high. The company never again paid a dividend on its ordinary shares.

Watkin attended the event in a wheelchair

The East London Railway

According to Watkin's original plan the line would pass from Baker Street along the Metropolitan tracks until it linked up with the third component, the East London Railway, also chaired by Sir Edward Watkin. This short length of track ran from New Cross, south of the river, to Shoreditch, with a connection to Great Eastern tracks at Liverpool Street. Its chief claim to distinction lay in the fact that it passed through the Thames Tunnel, the world's first tunnel to be built beneath a river. It had been designed by Marc Brunel and was the first to make use of a tunnelling shield, which has been the basis of tunnel construction ever since. Construction had begun in 1825 and was completed in 1843.[16] The 18 years which it took to complete the tunnel were marked by a series of disasters which included insolvency, flooding, several deaths and a near-fatal heart attack for Marc Brunel. When Marc later suffered a stroke his more famous son, Isambard, had taken over the project and himself narrowly escaped death in another accident. Although the completed tunnel was an object of great public interest it never made a profit. Its debts grew ever larger and it was with some relief that its unfortunate shareholders sold it to the East London Railway when the latter was formed in 1865.

The £200,000 which the railway paid was insufficient even to discharge the tunnel's debts and the railway itself was scarcely more successful. It opened in 1876 but never ran its own services, the locomotives and rolling stock being provided by other railway companies, one of them being Watkin's Metropolitan Railway. Within two years of opening the East London Railway had run into serious difficulties, partly as a result of placing its finances in the hands of a colourful and crooked financier called Albert Grant, who used some of the proceeds of his deception to restore Leicester Square.[17] This

Albert Grant, *né* Gottheimer, restorer of Leicester Square, who ruined the East London Railway. (By courtesy of the National Portrait Gallery, London)

an obstacle which had withstood the Spanish Armada and Napoleon would surely be no match for Sir Edward Watkin.

generosity with other people's money was appreciated by the citizens of London but did not help the wretched shareholders of the railway, who did as their counterparts on the Metropolitan had done and called in Sir Edward Watkin in 1878. Watkin rescued the line from its immediate problems and became its chairman, linking it to his Metropolitan Railway in 1884 and thus creating the next link in his chain. At New Cross it joined the South-Eastern Railway, also chaired by Watkin, which would take it to Folkestone. At this point it would meet the English Channel, but an obstacle which had withstood the Spanish Armada and Napoleon would surely be no match for Sir Edward Watkin.

'Vive le tunnel sous la Manche'

In 1875 a French company had been formed to finance a tunnel from the French side and in 1879 it had sunk an access shaft near the French village of Sangatte. In 1881 Watkin was one of the promoters of the Submarine Continental Railway Company which sank a shaft at Shakespeare Cliff between Dover and Folkestone close to the opening of the tunnel which was completed in 1994. Watkin informed the Board of Trade that the company would pay for one mile of tunnelling before seeking financial support from the Government, but any enthusiasm that Gladstone's parsimonious Government might have had for the project was forestalled by the Adjutant-General of the War Office, Sir Garnet Wolseley. He warned a Commission of Enquiry that 'a thousand men might easily come through the tunnel at night, avoiding all suspicion by being dressed as ordinary passengers, or passing at express speed through the tunnel with the blinds down, in their uniform and fully armed'.[18] Wolseley was supported in his opposition to the tunnel by a petition signed by such luminaries as Alfred, Lord Tennyson, the Archbishop of York and Cardinal Newman. To this spectre of a Trojan horse *Herapath's Railway Journal* added the fear that the cosmopolitan nature of the company would mean that 'many of the servants would probably be French' and that they would treacherously sabotage any attempt to defend the tunnel in the event of an invasion by their compatriots.[19] The French appear to have been the chief suspects at this time, though the Germans later took over this unenviable role. The Government agreed and told Watkin to cease his subterranean burrowing, its opposition being based on the legal precept that the Crown owned the foreshore. *Herapath's Railway Journal* reported the exchanges that followed as Watkin tried to overturn the prohibition. First he announced that 'the tunnel could be flooded in three minutes and a Minister in London, by pressing a button, could blow it up in a few seconds'. It may have occurred to some readers that the minister might turn out to be Sir Edward Watkin, MP, and the knowledge that such an irascible gentleman had the power to send them into the next world might have done little to reassure potential passengers.

In the face of these difficulties Watkin organised a stunt to gain public support for the enterprise. He brought to London Ferdinand de Lesseps, the distinguished French engineer who had built the Suez Canal. Amid much publicity de Lesseps emerged from Charing Cross station to be greeted by a phalanx of Watkin's employees from the South-Eastern Railway shouting in well-rehearsed French 'Vive la France! Vive le tunnel sous la Manche!'. A contemporary account of the occasion recorded that 'Naturally Monsieur de Lesseps went back to France with a passionate belief in the intelligence of the British working man'. De Lesseps, however, declined to be drawn into Watkin's scheme. On three separate occasions Watkin tried to introduce into Parliament a Bill which would authorize him to proceed with the tunnel, but repeated failure did not deter him from pressing on. He organized an excursion to Folkestone by train for MPs who then sat down to dinner in the partially excavated tunnel. At the annual meeting of the Submarine Company in 1890 Watkin announced that over 2,000 yards of tunnel had already been excavated. The suggestion that a bridge might be a simpler alternative was dismissed by Watkin, who said that 'the great advantage of making a tunnel was that they might afterwards make as many as they pleased'. He also spoke of the advantages of an onward link to Paris, the final stage in what the reporter described as Watkin's 'long-cherished dream'.[20] At the same meeting he proposed to build a

a thousand men might easily come through the tunnel at night

'Naturally Monsieur de Lesseps went back to France with a passionate belief in the intelligence of the British working man'

It could not be said of Sir Edward Watkin that he lacked determination

luxurious 'Metropolitan Grand Hotel' above the Metropolitan's headquarters at Moorgate station to accommodate the wealthy clientele who, according to Watkin's vision, could thus break their journeys on their passage from Manchester to Paris on the Watkin railway network. Shortly afterwards an insistent Government obliged him to stop and the tunnel project lapsed for another century. Watkin instead turned to digging for coal, an enterprise with which he persisted for another year in the hope that the Government would change its mind. He also advocated another railway tunnel between Scotland and Ireland. It could not be said of Sir Edward Watkin that he lacked determination.

SIR GARNET WOLSELEY (1833–1913)

Garnet Joseph Wolseley was born in Dublin in 1833, the son of a major. Wolseley's military career mirrored the fortunes of the

Victorian empire. He joined the army in 1852, fought in China and Burma and was decorated for his service before Sebastopol in the Crimean War. He distinguished himself in the Relief of Lucknow during the Indian Mutiny and later served at the War Office in London, where he actively promoted the reforms which transformed the British Army from an employment agency for the sons of the aristocracy to an efficient, professional force. He became a household name as the result of successful campaigns in Ghana and in the subjection of Zululand. He also suppressed a rebellion in Egypt which briefly threatened British control of the Suez Canal but in 1884 an expedition led by him failed to reach Khartoum in time to relieve the besieged General Gordon. Despite this setback he was created Viscount Wolseley in 1885 and in 1895 he became Commander-in-Chief of the British Army. His prestige as Britain's most celebrated soldier was influential in frustrating Sir Edward Watkin's plan for a Channel Tunnel. (Picture by courtesy of the National Portrait Gallery, London)

The beginnings of Metroland

The frustration of his grand vision of a railway from Manchester to Paris obliged Watkin to turn his attention to other plans which were, in the end, more lasting in their effects. He was correct in his belief that commuter traffic from what would later be called the suburbs would be more profitable than carriage of passengers within the metropolis. It was cheaper to build railways on the surface, across farmland, than to burrow beneath the streets of London and the area into which he now moved, north and west of London, was poorly served by main line railways. He was also able to take advantage of a provision in the Act of Parliament setting up the Metropolitan Railway, which was excluded from the Acts establishing other underground railways. It concerned the powers of the company to develop land. Such Acts gave the railway companies powers to purchase compulsorily the land over which they proposed to build the track, but the procedures for exercising such powers were frequently long-winded and expensive involving arbitration and, on occasion, appeals to the Home Secretary. Where possible therefore the companies tried to reach an accommodation with landowners. This might mean diverting the railway from the shortest route or it might involve the railway purchasing rather more land than it required. Thus if a track was to run through a field the farmer might agree to sell the whole field rather than be left with two small and divided portions. Once the line was completed the railway company would find itself with surplus land adjacent to its tracks and stations. This land had, of course, increased substantially in value since it was now suitable for housing.

The Acts establishing most of the underground railway companies specified that such surplus land should not be developed by the railways themselves, which were thus unable to benefit from the value they had helped to create. The land had to be offered for development either to the original owners or to third parties who reaped the rewards. In 1905 and again in 1938 representatives of the railway companies suggested that this prohibition be lifted so that the companies could recover some of the substantial capital investment which has always been an obstacle to investment in their infrastructure, but MPs were unimpressed, taking the view that the companies should concentrate on running the rail network rather than developing land. The Metropolitan Railway was the exception to this rule. Its Act did permit such development and in 1887 Watkin reconstituted the finances of the company, establishing its property interests as a separate enterprise from its railway operations. This was the origin of Metroland. In 1919 this became a fully fledged property company, Metropolitan Country Estates Ltd, which was in effect a subsidiary of the Metropolitan Railway.

The Watkin Tower

The creation of Metroland did not gather pace until after Watkin's death, but in the meantime he turned his attention to a more bizarre attempt to drum up passenger revenue from property development. He had been impressed by accounts he had read of the Paris Exhibition of 1889 and in particular by the success of the Eiffel Tower in attracting visitors to that event. He sent one of his engineers to view the tower and announced to his shareholders that the construction of such a tower adjacent to their railway would attract huge numbers of fare-paying visitors. He informed them that 'the Tower company have selected a site adjacent to your railway between Neasden and Harrow, upon which to erect their proposed Great Tower'. He could have mentioned that this convenient decision may have been influenced by the fact that he, Watkin, was the Tower Company's biggest share-holder, though the Metropolitan later bought £60,000 of its shares on Watkin's advice. Critics of his tower were subjected to the full blast of his vituperation. A shareholder called Turle who moved an amend-ment to the proposal was informed by Watkin that 'his amendment was about the most foolish he had ever heard a shareholder raise'.[21] When the resulting turmoil had subsided Watkin's proposal was passed. Watkin's shareholders' meetings were rarely dull affairs.

It was to be expected that a tower erected under the direction of Sir Edward Watkin would be superior to anything the French could produce so he formed a Metropolitan Tower Construction Company and invited architects from all over the world to submit designs for a tower higher than that of Gustave Eiffel. He gallantly invited the Frenchman to supervise the work which was supposed to dwarf his original design but the French engineer was no more enthusiastic about becoming involved in Watkin's schemes than his compatriot de Lesseps had been. In March 1890 the results of the competition were announced in *The Times*. Many of the entries were described as 'wildly extravagant, whilst others were marked by an entire absence of architectural merit'.[22] The prize was awarded to a 1,200-foot steel tower with two platforms and a small area at the top: very similar to the Eiffel Tower but gratifyingly higher. It would accommodate restaurants, theatres, a small ballroom, exhibitions and a Turkish bath.

In the regrettable absence of Gustave Eiffel the construction work was supervised by Sir Benjamin Baker, who had just finished constructing the Forth Railway Bridge. Work began in 1892 and was undertaken by the company that was, at the same time, building the

'his amendment was about the most foolish he had ever heard a shareholder raise'

It would accommodate restaurants, theatres, a small ballroom, exhibitions and a Turkish bath.

Blackpool Tower which, at 519 feet high, was less than half the size of Watkin's.

The first stage was reached in 1895, by which time the Blackpool Tower was complete, but Neasden did not have the same *cachet* as Paris or even Blackpool. The first visitors were admitted in May 1896 but, despite Watkin's confident predictions, the event passed almost unnoticed by the press or the public. The *Wealdstone, Harrow and Wembley Observer* divided its attention between the tower opening and the attractions of a nearby fête. The magistrates even turned down its application for a licence to sell alcohol. In the first year only 18,500 visitors paid to enter the attraction, using the new Wembley Park station that had been built to serve it. By this time ill health had compelled Watkin to retire, the announcement of his retirement causing the shares of his railway companies to register a rise in their value on the London Stock Exchange. The *Railway Times* marked his retirement by describing him as 'Masterful and capricious, talented and vain, sanguine and impetuous, he has at least shown himself with the courage of his convictions'.[23] He must have been grieved to see the fate that swiftly overtook his tower. In 1899 the Tower Company went into liquidation and thereafter the name 'Watkin's Folly' became cruelly attached to the crumbling edifice. The remains of the Watkin Tower were blown up in 1907 and 15 years later the site was used as a home for Wembley Stadium. Paradoxically this world-famous sporting venue generated far more traffic for the Metropolitan Railway's Wembley Park station than Watkin can ever have dreamed of.

Sir Edward Watkin died in 1901, two years after the opening of the London terminus at Marylebone on which he had set his heart. His obituary in the Manchester Guardian described him as 'a striking and masterful figure who leaves the rather dubious monument of having attempted to make a Channel Tunnel'. The *Times*[24] was more astringent. While acknowledging that Watkin was 'the railway king' of his age and more like an 'American boss' than a British railway chairman, it added that that 'his kingdom was, like the British Empire itself, built up of a number of disconnected entities with divergent and often conflicting interests'. Moreover 'the actual practical working of a railway was a subject he had never studied and never really understood', comparing his knowledge of such mundane matters unfavourably with 'any lad in the timetable office'. As for his 'fantastic schemes, the least said the better'. One of his fantastic schemes, the Watkin Tower, passed into history, almost forgotten. Sir Edward Watkin did not live to see the realisation of his more ambitious plans. It was only after 1918 that the development of Metroland created a

15 years later the site was used as a home for Wembley Stadium

'a striking and masterful figure who leaves the rather dubious monument of having attempted to make a Channel Tunnel'

more lasting monument to his plans for the Metropolitan railway. Ninety-three years would pass before his dream of a tunnel beneath the Channel would be realized. He died a frustrated visionary.

[1] The Charing Cross, Euston and Hampstead railway which Yerkes promoted was added to the City and South London Railway in 1924 to form what is now the Northern Line.

[2] *Herapath's Railway Journal*, August 1872, pages 884–5 give an account of the situation.

[3] And brother of the architect Alfred Waterhouse whose contribution to London is described in Chapter 8.

[4] Metropolitan Railway Minute Book, Metropolitan Archives, 1297, Met 1/4, pages 134–6.

[5] The Metropolitan Board of Works was London's first metropolitan government, which ran the affairs of London from 1856 to 1889. It was succeeded by the London County Council in 1889.

[6] Metropolitan Railway Minute Book, Metropolitan Archives, 1297, Met1/10, pages 499–500.

[7] Metropolitan Archives Acc.1297, Met. 1/13, page 461.

[8] *Railway Times,* 9 August 1884, page 1,000.

[9] *The Times*, 14 June 1879, page 8.

[10] Editor of the *Daily Mail* and later the *Daily Express*. The entry was made in *R.D.B.'s Diary*, for 23 June 1887.

[11] *Herapath's Railway Journal*, 20 July 1889, pages 789–90.

[12] Parliamentary papers, 1898, Vol.45, questions 429–30.

[13] *Underground to Everywhere*, S. Halliday, Sutton Publishing, 2001: Chapter 3 contains an account of Yerkes's contribution to the development of the London Underground.

[14] *The Times*, correspondence page, 5 December 1935 et seq.

[15] Metropolitan Archives, Board Minutes, Acc.1297, Met. 1/17, 14 January 1891.

[16] See Chapter 2 for an account of the building of the Thames Tunnel.

[17] See page 149 for an account of Albert Grant and his restoration of Leicester Square.

[18] Parliamentary papers, 1883, Vol.12; Wolseley gave his evidence on 21 June.

[19] *Herapath's Railway Journal*, 30 June 1888, page 742.

[20] *Herapath's Railway Journal*, 19 July 1890, page 823.

[21] *Railway Times,* 26 July 1890, page 94.

[22] *The Times*, 18 June 1890, page 10.

[23] *Railway Times*, 2 June 1894.

[24] *The Times*, 15 April 1901, page 6.

CHAPTER 8

Alfred Waterhouse and Victorian Gothic

'A True Temple of Nature, showing, as it should, the Beauty of Holiness.'
(*The Times*, April 1881, describing the Natural History Museum)

'More adapted for a suburban tea-garden than a national museum'.
(*The Field*, April, 1881, describing the Natural History Museum)

ALFRED Waterhouse was born on 19 July 1830 in Aigburth, Liverpool, to a family of wealthy Quakers. It was a talented family. His brother Edwin was a founding partner of the accountants Price Waterhouse and Alfred's son, Paul, was himself a distinguished architect who, by the time of his death in 1924, had established himself as a leading authority on town planning. The young Alfred was sent to a Quaker school in Tottenham, London, where he showed a gift for drawing and expressed an early wish to become an artist. His parents considered this occupation too frivolous for a Quaker so, as a compromise, he was articled in 1848, at the age of 18, to Richard Lane, the most prominent Manchester architect of his day. Alfred nevertheless retained his interest in art. He exhibited his first watercolour at the Royal Academy in 1857 and became an Academician in 1885. Alfred worked with Lane for five years but there is no reason to

Alfred Waterhouse. (By courtesy of the National Portrait Gallery, London)

suppose that he was much influenced by his master's views on architecture. Lane specialised in industrial buildings like factories and warehouses for Manchester cotton merchants, to which he relentlessly applied the classical and neo-classical designs which were in favour in the first half of the 19th century. Alfred Waterhouse reacted against this influence in his own work, a central feature of which was the revival of mediaeval, or Gothic, structures and ornamentation.

In June 1853, his articles completed, Alfred set out with his friend Thomas Hodgkin (whose sister he later married) on a Continental tour which lasted almost a year. He visited Rouen, Paris, Arles, Rome and Constantinople, making full use of his frustrated talents as an artist to fill numerous notebooks with drawings of buildings and their architectural details, each carefully described. In Constantinople he spent much time sketching Justinian's Aya Sophia, with its huge dome and columns, as well as the beautiful mosque of Sultan Suleiman; buildings which, in the mid-19th century, were little known in Britain. He appears to have been particularly intrigued by staircases, of which his notebooks contain many examples, notably an intricate drawing of the elaborate staircase in the Palazzo Barberini in Rome.

Upon his return to England in the summer of 1854, Alfred established his own architectural practice in Manchester, undertaking small commissions for local citizens, but the following year he returned to the Continent to visit the Paris exhibition of 1855. Again he filled his notebooks with sketches and comments. In Amiens, according to his notebook, he was 'much struck by the terracotta work – red brick being occasionally used in bands and arches for colour's sake'. This note is significant in view of the role that terracotta, and colour, were to play in his later work, notably at the Natural History Museum in South Kensington. The word 'terracotta' in Italian means, literally, 'cooked earth' – clay which has been baked to become durable and compact, often being cast in moulds to give decorative features. The technique dates from as early as the Stone Age, but its use declined in the late Middle Ages as the art of brickmaking was rediscovered. A further comment in the notebook Alfred kept during his Paris visit is also significant. He wrote: 'returned home much disgusted with English architecture. We want size, light and shade, and colour in our buildings'. These precepts all found expression in the designs that he went on to create.

'returned home much disgusted with English architecture'

The Gothic revival
At this time Alfred was becoming absorbed in the ideas of the Gothic revival. The expression 'gothic' was coined in Renaissance Italy to denote architecture which departed from classical norms. It was

intended as a pejorative term, the equivalent of 'barbaric'. In 18th-century England the word was still being used in this sense, to mean bizarre or tasteless, so Alfred Waterhouse was being far from conventional when he showed sympathy for mediaeval styles and techniques. He read widely the works of its most ardent advocates, such as John Ruskin (1819–1900) and Augustus Pugin (1812–52). He had read the former's *Seven Lamps of Architecture* (1849) and *Stones of Venice* (1851–3), which had marked Ruskin out as perhaps the most influential writer on architecture of the 19th century. In 1854 Ruskin had made the extravagant claim that 'it is the glory of Gothic architecture that it can do anything'. Ruskin particularly favoured the use of statuary on buildings for educational purposes, a technique of which Alfred was to make generous use at the Natural History Museum. Yet Ruskin was puritanically opposed to 'the use of cast or machine made ornaments of any kind' so it is not clear just how far his approval extended to the terracotta mouldings that decorate the exterior of the museum. Waterhouse also read Pugin's work *The True Principles of Pointed or Christian Architecture* (1841). Pugin, a Catholic convert, was mostly concerned with ecclesiastical architecture but he also designed some secular buildings, notably the Gothic mansion at Alton Towers, which was the home of the earls of Shrewsbury before it became one of Britain's principal leisure attractions. He was also responsible for the decoration and much of the sculpture in the Houses of Parliament, which were rebuilt in the 1840s and 1850s to the designs of Charles Barry.[1] Despite his growing enthusiasm for Gothic forms Waterhouse was critical of some of its more extravagant manifestations. Writing in his *Sketchbook* of Viollet-le-Duc's notorious 'restorations' of sites like Carcassone Waterhouse commented 'the energetic restorations now taking place through France are in too many cases re-building'.[2]

Ruskin and Pugin had other disciples whose buildings and writings reflected contemporary attitudes to the introduction of mediaeval or Gothic features to Victorian architecture. Barry and Pugin had designed the New Palace of Westminster in the Gothic style specified by the Select Committee that commissioned the design. George Gilbert Scott (1811–78), later the designer of St Pancras station and George Edmund Street (1824–81), whose design was later chosen in preference to Waterhouse's for the Law Courts in the Strand, had both studied Continental mediaeval architecture. They suggested that it had much to offer while expressing reservations about its wholesale use in an English context. John Parker (1806–84), author of *An Introduction to the Study of Gothic Architecture* (1849) and first keeper of the Ashmolean Museum, Oxford, engaged in a controversy with Street in

Pugin designed some secular buildings, notably the Gothic mansion at Alton Towers

'the energetic restorations now taking place through France are in too many cases re-building'

JOHN RUSKIN (1819–1900)

John Ruskin was the most influential art critic of his time. Born in 1819, the son of a wine merchant, he was a published poet by the age of 15 and later gained an MA at Oxford. He became a friend of J.M.W. Turner, whom he defended in *Modern Painters* and supported the Pre-Raphaelites in their return to naturalistic styles of painting. He described great art as 'the expression of a mind of a God-made man'. Like Pugin he advocated mediaeval styles of architecture and attacked the effects of industrialisation on the working classes, for whom he actively promoted art education and public museums. He criticised the efforts of Henry Cole and others to apply the principles of good design to mass production, writing that 'Sir Henry Cole at Kensington has corrupted the teaching of art-education all over England into a state of abortion and falsehood from which it will take twenty years to recover'. His publications *The Stones of Venice* and *The Seven Lamps of Architecture* exercised a profound influence on attitudes to architecture and painting as did his monthly *Letters to the Workmen and Labourers of Great Britain*. He taught at the Working Men's College in London where he enlisted Dante Gabriel Rossetti to help him. His ideas inspired the Arts and Crafts Movement, the founders of the National Trust and William Morris's Society for the Protection of Ancient Buildings. His unconsummated marriage to his young bride Effie Gray was annulled in 1855. In 1871 he went to live at Brantwood, on Coniston Water in the Lake District, where he died in 1900.

the columns of the influential magazine *The Builder*,[3] which sums up the orthodoxy of the time. Referring to Street and his followers Parker wrote: 'let them study the buildings of the whole world but that is no reason for importing details from Lombardy and introducing them into English buildings'. By this date the Gothic New Palace of Westminster was nearing completion and Parker's cause was lost. Alfred Waterhouse would shortly emphasise the triumph of Victorian Gothic in his most celebrated design.

that is no reason for importing details from Lombardy and introducing them into English buildings'

Manchester Assize Courts

In 1859 Waterhouse entered the competition for the design for new assize courts in Manchester. Before preparing his submission he travelled to Belgium, observing and sketching municipal buildings in Bruges, Antwerp, Brussels and Ypres. He later wrote of his winning design that 'the mouldings and details are thirteenth century in their general character. But wherever I thought that the particular object in view could not best be obtained by strict adherence to precedent I took the liberty of departing from it'.[4] The design was widely applauded despite continuing reservations in some quarters about Continental and Gothic features. The assize courts' magnificent beamed hall echoed the finest mediaeval structures, while its roof of coloured, patterned tiles, reminiscent of the magnificent roofs of Burgundy, was a most unusual and striking feature in English architecture.[5] Waterhouse was now recognised as an architect of the first rank. He moved his practice to London where he occupied premises at 20 (now 67) New Cavendish Street and, as a direct result of his success in Manchester, attracted many more commissions. The Manchester Assize Courts particularly impressed Emily Davies, founder of Girton College, Cambridge. She wrote to her friend Anna Richardson: 'I don't think I told you how much we enjoyed the beauty of the Assize Courts. I have seen no modern building to be compared with it'. She later employed Waterhouse for three decades in the design and construction of Girton.

The new museum

It was as a result of his successful design for the Manchester Assize Courts that, in 1866, Alfred Waterhouse was invited to take over responsibility for the new Natural History Museum in South Kensington. The project already had a long history. Technically the Natural History Museum was (and remained until 1963) the natural history department of the British Museum. It originated in the will of Sir Hans Sloane (1660–1753), a prominent London physician who had devoted his life to assembling a unique collection, ranging from dried plants and animal skeletons to artefacts from the ancient world. He offered his collection to the Crown for £20,000, but stipulated that it should 'remain together, and not be separated, and that chiefly in and about the city of London, where I have acquired most of my estates and where they may by the great confluence of people most be used'. Parliament agreed to these terms and in 1756 Sloane's collection moved into Montagu House in Bloomsbury, the first home of the British Museum. Over the next century the collection grew through the acquisition of notable specimens, the most important being those gathered by Joseph Banks during his voyage to the South Seas in 1768 with Captain Cook on the *Endeavour*. By the 19th century the collection had outgrown its modest share of the space available on the Bloomsbury site.

Richard Owen – whose determined advocacy led to the creation of the Natural History Museum.

In 1856 responsibility for the collection fell upon professor Richard Owen (1804–92) who was appointed as superintendent of the British Museum's department of natural history. Owen was a celebrated palaeontologist who gave us the word 'dinosaur'. He at once set about campaigning for new accommodation but was not assisted in his efforts by his unusual gift for antagonising people who would have been useful as allies. In 1851 Thomas Huxley had written of Owen 'It is astonishing with what an intense feeling of hatred Owen is regarded

'It is astonishing with what an intense feeling of hatred Owen is regarded by the majority of his contemporaries'

by the majority of his contemporaries. The truth is that he is the superior of most and does not conceal that he knows it'. However Owen was not always right and was especially wrong in his judgement of the greatest of all naturalists, Charles Darwin. In the famous debate on Darwin's theory of evolution, which took place at Oxford in 1859, Owen supplied Samuel Wilberforce, Bishop of Oxford, with much of the material for his anti-Darwinian arguments, which Thomas Huxley, 'Darwin's Bulldog', effortlessly demolished.

THOMAS HUXLEY (1825–95)

Thomas Huxley's early career bore some similarity to that of the man he most admired, Charles Darwin, though he did not come from a wealthy family as Darwin did. Just as Darwin had joined the Royal Navy Ship HMS *Beagle* for his historic voyage to the Galapagos Islands, Huxley joined HMS *Rattlesnake,* which charted the seas around Australia and New Guinea from 1846. The species that he collected and analysed on this voyage won him recognition amongst the London scientific community and he became friendly with Darwin and with William Hooker.[6] He supported himself and his wife (whom he had met in Sydney, Australia) in a modest lifestyle by writing articles of popular science and lecturing at the School of Mines in London. Upon reading Darwin's *Origin of Species* he exclaimed 'How stupid of me not to have thought of that myself!' His moment of fame came at the meeting of the British Association at Oxford in 1860. Bishop Samuel Wilberforce, coached by Richard Owen, attacked Darwin's theories. Huxley, who had read and been thoroughly convinced by Darwin's great work, demolished Wilberforce's arguments. Henceforth Huxley was known as 'Darwin's Bulldog'. He gave us the word 'agnostic' to describe one who is neither a believer nor an atheist and founded a remarkable intellectual dynasty. His descendants include Sir Andrew Huxley, a Nobel prize-winner; the writer Julian Huxley; and the author of *Brave New World*, Aldous Huxley.

Nevertheless, Owen's authority carried considerable weight in his field and in 1858 he persuaded 120 eminent scientists to sign a petition to Disraeli, Chancellor of the Exchequer, requesting that resources be found to create accommodation more suitable for the natural history collection. Nothing resulted from this petition so in 1861 Owen took the further step of giving William Gladstone, the Chancellor of the new Liberal Government, a conducted tour of the collection. Owen took advantage of every opportunity to draw the attention of the statesman-scholar to the inadequacies of the accommodation. Owen himself suggested to the trustees of the British Museum that the physical limitations of the Bloomsbury site were such that a move to a new, separate museum was inevitable. He recommended a huge museum in what was then the undeveloped suburb of Kensington. The site he had in mind had been part of the land acquired by the Commissioners of the Great Exhibition of 1851 and had been purchased with the £186,000 profits made by that remarkable event.[7] The whole site stretched from the present site of the Albert Memorial south to the Cromwell Road and is now occupied by a complex of buildings which include the Albert Hall, the Science Museum, Imperial College, the Royal College of Organists, the Victoria and Albert Museum and the Natural History Museum. At the time of Owen's campaign it was mostly occupied by the buildings and gardens of the Royal Horticultural Society. The most prominent building on the site, however, was a large and hideous corrugated iron shed which contained exhibits that later found a home in the Science Museum. Officially known as 'The Iron Museum' it was celebrated for its ugliness and became known as 'The Brompton Boilers'. When questioned about the wisdom of leaving Bloomsbury for this distant and unloved part of London Owen replied 'I love Bloomsbury much but I love five acres more'.

That part of the site which Owen wanted amounted to about five acres and was occupied by a building erected for the later, less successful exhibition of 1862. This had been designed by Captain Francis Fowke (1823–65) of the Royal Engineers, and had been described by the influential magazine *The Builder* as 'one of the ugliest public buildings that was ever raised in this country'. Owen was therefore on sure ground in requiring the demolition of Fowke's despised building, but the Parliamentary Committee which scrutinised his proposal was alarmed by the scale of the building with which Owen proposed to replace it, amounting to almost half a million square feet: 10 times the space his collection occupied at Bloomsbury. He proposed to house related species together in huge galleries surrounding a nave-like centre, which he called an 'index museum'. This museum within a museum would house species which were representative of those in the galleries. Thus the skeleton of a whale would represent the largest mammal while the giraffe would represent the tallest. It was anticipated that the visitors' interest would be aroused by the spectacular specimens in the 'index' and that they would thereby be encouraged to visit the related specimens in the galleries. The parliamentarians were not impressed, commenting 'An exhibition on so large a scale tends alike to the needless bewilderment and fatigue of

'one of the ugliest public buildings that was ever raised in this country'

the public and the impediment of the studies of the scientific visitor'. The MP for Galway, Sir William Gregory, husband of the Lady Gregory who was shortly to play such a prominent part in the revival of the Irish theatre, lamented the fact that 'a man [Richard Owen] whose name stood so high should connect himself with so foolish, crazy and extravagant a scheme'. Perhaps Owen was simply aiming high, assuming that, by asking for more than he could hope to get, he would be granted something that would meet his minimum needs.

An embarrassing winner

In 1863 a portion of the site was acquired by Act of Parliament, the offending 1862 structure was demolished and a competition was announced for the design for the new museum. Entries for the competition were submitted anonymously to a panel of architects and by a bizarre twist the prize was awarded to Captain Francis Fowke, the very same architect that had designed the despised, and recently demolished, pavilion for the 1862 exhibition. He had also been responsible for another prominent building on the site, the Royal Horticultural Society's conservatory. Fowke's success had aroused the envy of the architectural profession, which did not think it right that a military engineer should enjoy so much success in designing public buildings. For this reason Fowke was never elected a member of the Royal Institute of British Architects. It was fortunate for Fowke that entries for the design competition were anonymous. It must have been galling for the architects when they discovered the identity of the man to whom they had awarded the palm. Fowke's design for the new museum was classical in conception and this is the museum that would no doubt have been built if it were not for the fact that, in 1865, Fowke died, probably from overwork. As well as designing the new museum Fowke had been working on a model of the proposed Albert Hall.

Faced with the untimely demise of their architect the trustees approached Alfred Waterhouse, the now celebrated architect of the much-admired Manchester Assize Courts, which were by this time in course of construction. Waterhouse could hardly decline such a prestigious (and eventually lucrative) commission but the increasingly confident advocate of the Gothic revival was now faced with the prospect of executing another architect's classical design.

In March 1868, Waterhouse submitted his proposed design for the new museum. It was radically different from Fowke's. In Waterhouse's own words he 'abandoned the idea of a Renaissance building and fell back on the earlier Romanesque style which prevailed largely in Lombardy and the Rhineland from the tenth to the end of the twelfth century'.[8] So much for John Parker's objections to importations from

Lombardy.[9] Waterhouse's experience was the mirror image of that of George Gilbert Scott at the Foreign Office. Ten years earlier Scott had designed a building in the English Gothic style and had been instructed by the Foreign Secretary, Palmerston, to alter it to a Renaissance building. On that occasion the classical school triumphed but Waterhouse was ready with arguments in support of the Romanesque design that he proposed. With the support of Richard Owen, whose brainchild the museum was, Waterhouse argued that the exterior of the building should be decorated with representations of the birds and beasts that were to be found within, these serving an educational purpose as advocated by Ruskin. Such figures were a feature of mediaeval buildings, as found on the great cathedrals. They were less well suited to the classical columns and façade of Fowke's design. A concession was made to the classical style in the symmetrical layout of the building, with towers on either side of the main entrance and at the end of the east and west wings.

the exterior of the building should be decorated with representations of the birds and beasts

A diversion: the Victoria Embankment

A change of government now intervened and in December 1868 the new Liberal Government, with Gladstone as prime minister, proposed a complete change of plan. At this time Sir Joseph Bazalgette's Victoria Embankment was nearing completion.[10] This magnificent structure, stretching a mile and a half from Westminster Bridge to Blackfriars Bridge, was created to solve five of the most pressing problems that faced the capital. Firstly, it reclaimed 37 acres of land from the Thames, which at that time was the receptacle of all of London's sewage, making the river deeper, faster and hence cleaner. Secondly, it provided a route for Bazalgette's main sewer, which intercepted the sewage from north of the river and conducted it, by gravity, to the treatment works at Barking. Thirdly, it provided a fine new road from Westminster to the City to relieve the hopelessly congested Strand–Fleet Street–Ludgate Hill route. Fourthly, it was built to accommodate the new underground railway, now the District and Circle Line. Finally, it provided 15 acres of much-needed open space in that congested part of London, in the form of Victoria Embankment Gardens. Gladstone, however, saw other possibilities. He proposed to build offices on Bazalgette's reclaimed land, these to be let at a substantial profit to the Crown. At this time he was still hoping to abolish the income tax which had been introduced as a 'temporary' measure by William Pitt during the Napoleonic Wars, and the office rents were part of Gladstone's plan to achieve this worthy if unlikely aim. In this he was thwarted by the stationer-statesman W.H. Smith, who organised protest meetings, a petition to the Queen and a debate

he was thwarted by the stationer-statesman W.H. Smith, who organised protest meetings, a petition to the Queen and a debate in Parliament

in Parliament in his capacity as MP for Westminster. Smith argued that Victoria Embankment Gardens should be retained as an open space. Gladstone, with great reluctance, dropped the office plan but countered by proposing that the embankment would be an eminently suitable site for the new museum. Waterhouse duly produced a design which would follow the curve of the river.

Back to South Kensington

In May 1870, two months before the Victoria Embankment was opened, Gladstone finally abandoned his designs on Bazalgette's new structure and reverted to the South Kensington site. However, he now presented Waterhouse with another problem in the person of Acton Smee Ayrton (1816–86), whom he appointed First Commissioner for Works, in which capacity he was responsible for public buildings. Ayrton, a lawyer by profession, yielded nothing to his master, Gladstone, in his enthusiasm for low taxation and economy in public works. It is hard to disagree with the judgement of Mark Girouard, historian of the museum, that 'Ayrton's main passion was for economy; he despised art, disliked most architects and artists, and felt that one of his main functions was to cut them down to size'.[11] For these tendencies he earned Sir John Betjeman's description of him as 'that stinker Ayrton'. Even Waterhouse's legendary charm failed to overcome Ayrton's hostility. One of Ayrton's first acts was to cut Waterhouse's budget for the new museum from £500,000 to £330,000. Faced with the loss of one third of his budget, Waterhouse redesigned the museum so that, instead of the 'E' shape he had planned, it simply comprised two wings radiating from a central, nave-like hall: a 'T' shape. He intended that the top and bottom arms of the 'E' should be added later when a less parsimonious mood prevailed. In the event they were never built. As a further cost-saving measure he cut the height of the two central towers on either side of the entrance so that they were the same height as the towers at the end of the east and west wings. We have Captain Shaw, chief of the London Fire Brigade, to thank for the fact that the two central towers were restored to their original height. The towers accommodated the cisterns which were to supply water for the building and Shaw insisted that they be built to the planned height in order to generate sufficient pressure for his hoses. In a final measure to meet the restrictions of Ayrton's budget, Waterhouse omitted the planned library and lecture theatre. The latter facility would have been an unusual and enlightened feature of a museum at the time and a further 80 years elapsed before the library and lecture theatre were added. A delay in inviting tenders which was caused by the leisurely pace at which the 'stinker Ayrton'

he earned Sir John Betjeman's description of him as 'that stinker Ayrton'

considered Waterhouse's plans meant that the contracts were not let until 1872, by which date building costs had escalated owing to the amount of building work which was going on in London at the time.

Building began in the spring of 1879 and proceeded reasonably smoothly until the main contractors, Baker and Son, went bankrupt, complaining loudly that their problems were caused in part by changes to the design made by Waterhouse as the work progressed. The creditors of the bankrupt builder sued for alterations to the contract and were awarded £25,000 compensation, but they allowed the work to proceed and the museum opened in 1881. The final cost of the building was £412,000, plus Waterhouse's fee of £19,730. The new museum was widely applauded. It consisted of a huge central nave-like main hall, the two towers on either side of the entrance matched by two smaller ones at the rear of the 'nave'. The visitor entered through a magnificent recessed polychromic doorway built in the Romanesque style and reminiscent of that at Le Puy, in France, which Waterhouse visited in 1872, while completing the design details. The doorway was reached by an imposing double staircase, which led the visitor to a hall 52 metres long and 22 metres high. The visitor's eye was drawn to the brilliantly painted ceiling and to another ornate staircase, more Baroque than mediaeval, at the far end of the hall, which led to the upper floors. The public never saw the two figures at the foot of the great staircase, which had been the object of protesting press correspondence led by a Mr Newton, who complained that they would 'corrupt and degrade public taste'. They were removed. It is assumed that they were nude figures for which the Victorian citizenry were not yet ready.[12] The external walls were structural but the interior of the building was carried on an iron frame which was exposed to reflect the technological advances of the industrial revolution, reminiscent of the great railway stations of the time.

'That stinker Ayrton' whose penny-pinching obliged Waterhouse to reduce the scale of his design for the museum. (By courtesy of the National Portrait Gallery, London)

'A true Temple of Nature'
In the month of its opening *The Saturday Review* praised 'Mr

The 'Index' museum.

Le Puy in London – museum doorway.

many of the drawings of living species were taken from the work of the greatest naturalist of all

Waterhouse's beautiful Romanesque building' while *The Times*, with an extravagant display of capital letters, portentously declared that citizens 'will now have the opportunity of pursuing the most delightful of all studies in a True Temple of Nature, showing, as it should, the Beauty of Holiness'.[13] The newspaper liked the terracotta figures of animals, including 50 extinct species on the eastern façade and living species on the western façade. Waterhouse had created these from drawings supplied by Richard Owen since the latter told his son that 'I took the liberty to suggest that many objects of Natural History might afford subjects for architectural ornament; and at Mr Waterhouse's request I transmitted numerous figures of such as seemed suitable for that purpose'. It is likely that many of the drawings of living species were taken from the work of the greatest naturalist of all. Owen had supervised the publication of Charles Darwin's seminal work *Zoology of the Voyage of HMS Beagle* before falling out with Darwin over the theory of evolution. Many of the museum's terracotta figures are of species illustrated in Darwin's *Beagle* account.

The museum typified features which were to become hallmarks of Waterhouse's designs in the years that followed: strong skylines; bold use of colour in brick, stone and terracotta; and spectacular staircases and doorways where space permitted. A further advantage of terracotta was that it could be cleaned relatively easily at a time when the prevailing atmosphere of London was that of soot. In 1891, in a lecture to students at the Royal Institute of British Architects, Waterhouse informed his audience that 'architects must look upon soot as a factor whose alliance they must do their best to defeat'. On a later occasion he told an audience in Birmingham that as terracotta was 'made from a clay found in the same pit as the coal that did the mischief, it seems the only building material which can successfully withstand its corroding influence'. Waterhouse was a founder member of the Smoke Abatement Society and his use of the soot-resistant terracotta was triumphantly vindicated 100 years after the museum opened when the façade was cleaned and restored in the 1980s.[14]

The building did not gain universal approval and there were some problems with the design. The positioning of staircases at each end of the central hall made it impractical to pass from one gallery to another without returning to the central hall. The central 'index' museum was not the success that had been hoped. Opposition from some of the keepers of the various collections made them reluctant to entrust their prize specimens to the 'museum within the museum' though the 'nave' later became the ideal repository for spectacular reconstructions of dinosaurs which cannot fail to strike the visitor upon entry. The still controversial nature of this early example of Victorian Gothic was reflected in *The Field*, which criticized the 'incorrect and grotesque representations of animals ... more adapted for a suburban tea-garden than a national museum'.[15] In 1894 August Hare's *Walks in London* described it as 'a huge pile of Lombardic architecture' and as late as 1962 Pevsner declared that 'The building is of a crushing symmetry ... forbidding and terribly serious' adding that terracotta was 'the least appealing of materials, of a soapy hardness and impermeable to weather'. The last criticism is particularly strange since the façade's resistance to London's notorious smogs would be regarded by most as advantageous. A later edition of Pevsner's work modified this judgement, conceding that the cleaning of the façade in the 1970s had revealed 'surprisingly delicate shades of buff and grey-blue'.[16] The more sympathetic John Betjeman described Waterhouse as 'a practical North Countryman with drive and charm and more sensibility than he is credited with'.[17]

Demolish Sir Christopher Wren's chapel!

The Manchester Assize Courts had drawn attention to Waterhouse's work. The Natural History Museum made his name and helped to establish the Victorian Gothic style which it most splendidly represented. Many further commissions followed, notably from Oxford and Cambridge colleges. During the early stages of the museum's construction he executed one of his finest small designs in the form of a new library for Pembroke College, Cambridge, but his work at Pembroke, which ended amid much controversy, demonstrates that his loyalty was to the Victorian version of mediaeval

'architects must look upon soot as a factor whose alliance they must do their best to defeat'.

'a practical North Countryman with drive and charm and more sensibility than he is credited with'

architecture rather than to the original. In the 1870s, Pembroke and other Cambridge colleges awoke from the long slumber of the late 18th and early 19th century to the opportunities presented by the Victorian educational reforms. Undergraduate numbers grew rapidly and the Master and Fellows of Pembroke invited Waterhouse to suggest 'the best way of providing for the college a group of buildings, as efficient, convenient and architecturally effective as the site was capable of'.[18] He built a new residential building called 'Red Buildings': a red-brick building in French Renaissance style with a high tower; and a fine library in Continental Gothic style with a Belgian-style clock tower. Waterhouse's further plans involved demolishing virtually the entire mediaeval college together with Pembroke's celebrated chapel, the first ever designed by Christopher Wren. Waterhouse regarded the proposed destruction of this gem as 'a matter of regret' though he judged that its style was bad and it was awkwardly situated. Waterhouse was attracted by the opportunity to replace it with an Italianate campanile 'sufficiently high to be the most conspicuous tower in Cambridge, which suffers from the lack of lofty architectural features'. The nervous Fellows drew the line at this act of vandalism but did allow Waterhouse to demolish the college's mediaeval hall, despite a campaign in *The Times* by a formidable team of bishops, headmasters and professors, all graduates of Pembroke. The demolition was partly justified by the assertion that the hall was structurally unsound. Some doubt was cast on this verdict by the impressive quantity of explosive material that was required to bring down the obstinate edifice. Waterhouse duly replaced the mediaeval hall with his own design, but by now his plans for Pembroke's

Waterhouse's further plans involved demolishing virtually the entire mediaeval college together with Pembroke's celebrated chapel, the first ever designed by Christopher Wren

Waterhouse's library and 'Red Buildings' at Pembroke College, Cambridge. One of Cambridge's jewels, the Wren chapel, may be seen to the right of the picture, having survived Waterhouse's plan to demolish it!

remaining buildings had alarmed the Fellows and an opposition group, whose activities were recorded in the diaries of a Fellow called John Neville Keynes[19] put an end to Waterhouse's work at Pembroke. He was informed by the college treasurer that 'Having resolved to keep the old college buildings we think it best to apply to someone whose style is specially conservative'. The choice fell upon George Gilbert Scott and Waterhouse was offended by the implication that he was not sufficiently conservative. Waterhouse was a founder member of the Society for the Preservation of Ancient Buildings, a fact that would no doubt have surprised the Master and Fellows of Pembroke.

'Find out exactly what is wanted'.
By the time the Natural History Museum opened Waterhouse had designed Manchester University and Manchester Town Hall, together with Liverpool University, where his extensive use of red bricks gave rise to the condescending expression 'red-brick' to describe the great civic universities of the late 19th and early 20th century.[20] In 1889, in his presidential address to students of the RIBA, Waterhouse described his approach to architecture. He told them: 'First find out exactly what is wanted; never think about the elevation of your building till you have ascertained this and embodied it in your plans as fully and perfectly as you can'. This 'modernist' approach to architecture helps to explain the large number of commercial buildings he was invited to design in addition to prestigious commissions such as University College Hospital and the National Liberal Club. His most loyal client was the Prudential Assurance company, for whom he designed 22 buildings, including, most notably, the head office in Holborn which he completed in 1879. The last has been described as 'a serious piece of Gothic renaissance knocked up by Sir [sic] Alfred Waterhouse'[21] though it has now been renamed 'Holborn Bars' to reflect the fact that the Prudential Assurance company has moved to a less distinctive building in the city. The knighthood mistakenly attributed to Waterhouse in this quotation from *The Guardian* was offered but never in fact conferred by the Queen. Waterhouse declined the honour on the grounds that all his designs were the result of teamwork and that the acceptance of a knighthood by himself would not do justice to the work of others.

In 1963, by Act of Parliament, the Natural History Museum was separated from its parent, the British Museum, and given its own board of trustees. In 1986 the adjacent Geological Museum was incorporated in the Natural History Museum, which had become firmly established as one of the world's great museums. It is also one of the finest examples of Victorian Gothic architecture and helped to

the acceptance of a knighthood by himself would not do justice to the work of others

Waterhouse's striking 'Prudential' building, now known as 'Holborn Bars'. (By courtesy of the Guildhall Library, Corporation of London)

'he did more than almost any other individual to establish the standard architectural dress of the late nineteenth century town'

establish a pattern that was being followed in many contemporary buildings. Apart from Waterhouse's own designs they include George Gilbert Scott's St Pancras Station Hotel (1874) and Albert Memorial (1876); and G.E. Street's Law Courts (1882) for which Waterhouse himself submitted a design.

In 1887 *Building News* ran a poll to select the leading British architect and Alfred Waterhouse won 90 percent of the votes. A later historian has suggested that 'he did more than almost any other individual to establish the standard architectural dress of the late nineteenth century town'.[22] By the time of his death in 1905 his approach to architecture had become temporarily unfashionable, as reflected in his obituary in *The Times*, which recorded that 'it would be affectation to ignore the fact that among the younger school of architects Mr Waterhouse's architecture was not regarded with favour and sympathy' though the writer added that Waterhouse was 'One of the most genial and attractive of men … even those who did not like his architecture loved the man'. As Victorian architecture has returned to favour many more now like the architecture as well as appreciating the architect.

[1] See Chapter 5 for an account of the work of Barry and Pugin in the rebuilt Houses of Parliament.

[2] *Sketchbook*, 1855–6, page 26.

[3] *The Builder*, 15 January 1859, page 45.

[4] *Building News*, 15 April 1859, page 365.

[5] Waterhouse's Manchester Assize Courts were bomb-damaged during World War Two and demolished shortly afterwards.

[6] See page 82 for an account of the work of William Hooker.

[7] *King Cole: a Picture Portrait of Sir Henry Cole, 1808–82* by Elizabeth Bonython, published by the Victoria & Albert Museum, gives an account of the events and personalities surrounding this event.

[8] *The Natural History Museum at South Kensington, 1753–1980*, W.T. Stearn, Natural History Museum, 1998, page 45.

[9] See page 174 above.

[10] See Chapter 6 for an account of Sir Joseph Bazalgette's work in London.

[11] *Alfred Waterhouse and the Natural History Museum*; Mark Girouard, Natural History Museum, 1999, page 22.

[12] *Alfred Waterhouse and the Natural History Museum*; Mark Girouard, Natural History Museum, 1999, page 23 describes this episode.

[13] *The Times*, 18 April 1881.

[14] This aspect of Waterhouse's work is described in *Alfred Waterhouse, 1830–1905*, Sally Maltby et al., 1983, pages 44 et seq.

[15] *The Field*, 28 April 1881.

[16] *London North-West*, Penguin, 1991, ed. Bridget Cherry.

[17] *A Pictorial History of English Art*, John Betjeman, John Murray, 1972, page 93.

[18] *Pembroke College Cambridge, a Celebration* ed. A.V. Grimstone, 1999, page 112, describes the episode and is the principal source of the account which follows.

[19] Father of the economist John Maynard Keynes.

[20] The expression 'red-brick' was first used in 1943 by a professor of Liverpool University.

[21] *The Guardian*, 13 March 2001.

[22] *Alfred Waterhouse, 1830–1905*, Sally Maltby et al. published in 1983 to accompany an exhibition of Waterhouse's drawings at the Royal Institute of British Architects.

Epilogue

The Vacant Plinth

FOR more than three years a committee presided over by Sir John Mortimer has considered the claims of historical figures, contemporary personalities, fictional characters and works of art to occupy the vacant plinth in Trafalgar Square. Winnie the Pooh and a stiletto shoe have been suggested as suitable candidates and a figure of David Beckham actually made it for a few hours during the World Cup of 2002. The plinth was originally intended as a home for a statue of William IV, but when that improvident monarch made way for his niece, Victoria, in 1837, there were insufficient funds in the royal coffers to pay for the monument. It has now been decided that the vacant plinth will be occupied by a series of temporary exhibits or monuments.

Who, then, should share Trafalgar Square with the one king (George IV) and two soldiers on the other three plinths, not to mention the rather better-known sailor on his column? Is it not fitting that the men whose achievements are celebrated in this book, and who did so much to create Victoria's London, should have their spell on the plinth? They inherited a disorderly collection of parishes and left us the first world city. What, then, are the claims of each of them?

John Nash, by constructing his 'New Street' from Regent's Park to St James's, could be said to have created the idea of the 'West End' of London, distinct from its business district. Moreover, it was he who proposed the laying out of Trafalgar Square itself, as well as Piccadilly Circus. **Charles Barry** designed one of London's, and the world's, most famous buildings in the Palace of Westminster, as well as laying out the terrace to the north of Trafalgar Square on which the National Gallery stands. They both deserve a few months on the plinth. **Marc Brunel,** unlike his famous son Isambard, is not well served by public monuments in London or elsewhere. His development of the tunnelling shield enabled London to have its tube railways, without which life in the metropolis would be impossible. **Thomas Cubitt,** perhaps the least well known of the figures in this volume, turned waterlogged fields and foetid swamps into good homes for the aristocracy, the middle and artisan classes at a time when less enlightened builders were creating slum tenements. These two deserve a spell on the plinth because they made it possible for Victorian Londoners to live and move in a civilised manner.

Sir Joseph Paxton's great monument was, of course, the Crystal Palace itself, and it was not his fault that it went up in flames in 1936. The profits generated by the Great Exhibition in 'Paxton's Palace' paid for the land on which **Alfred Waterhouse** built the Natural History Museum, thus creating the museums district of South Kensington, which is one of London's greatest glories. Perhaps they should share the plinth for a few months. **Sir Edward Watkin** tried to create his own grandiose monument in the Watkin Tower at Neasden but no one was sorry when it was blown up after his death. On the other hand, he did begin the process of creating Metroland, that archetype of suburban living which is sometimes derided but is celebrated in Betjeman's verse. Without such suburbs most Londoners would have nowhere to live. Perhaps he deserves a few weeks on the plinth.

The final candidate is **Sir Joseph Bazalgette**. Without his drains, sewers, pumping stations and treatment works, which continue to serve London more than a century after his death, tens of thousands more Londoners would have been wiped out in epidemics of cholera and typhoid as they were in Hamburg and elsewhere in Europe. The victims would no doubt have included the ancestors of many of the readers of this book. Moreover, the site in Trafalgar Square would be especially suitable for Bazalgette. Looking towards the river down Northumberland Avenue, which he built, he would be able to glimpse another of his creations, the Victoria Embankment, which houses the greatest of his intercepting sewers as well as the underground railway. Behind his left shoulder would be another of his great works, Charing Cross Road, the construction of which caused him to demolish some of the worst slums in London at St Giles. His most substantial monument in London is a small bust set into the wall of the Victoria Embankment. He has, perhaps, the strongest claim of all to the first and longest spell on the vacant plinth.

Further Reading

SOME of the subjects of this volume have not been well served by recent biographers. **John Nash** in particular is a rather neglected subject and **Charles Barry**, while celebrated in the 19th century by writers and lecturers who remembered him, has yet to find a later biographer to do full justice to his work.

Books on **Isambard Kingdom Brunel** are legion. This author particularly recommends *Isambard Kingdom Brunel, Engineering Knight-Errant*, by Adrian Vaughan, published by John Murray, 1991, as a good short account of his eventful life, as is the classic *Isambard Kingdom Brunel*, by L.T.C. Rolt, Penguin, 1989. Works on **Marc Brunel** are harder to come by but *Brunel's Tunnel*, by A. Mathewson and D. Laval, published in 1992, is a good short account of his life and work. It is available from the Brunel Exhibition, Railway Avenue, Rotherhithe, London SE16. *The Triumphant Bore*, published by the Institution of Civil Engineers in 1993 and available from the Institution's bookshop in Great George Street, SW1, may also be recommended.

The definitive account of **Thomas Cubitt's** life and work is by Hermione Hobhouse: *Thomas Cubitt, Master Builder*, published by Macmillan in 1971 and republished by Management Books in 1995. J. Summerson's *Georgian London*, Barrie & Jenkins, 1988, contains references to Cubitt's work in the early part of the 19th century. A good short account of the life and work of **Sir Joseph Paxton** is to be found in *Joseph Paxton*, by John Anthony, Shire Publications, 1973, while *Paxton's Palace*, by Anthony Bird, Cassell, 1976, gives a more detailed analysis of the Crystal Palace itself. The background to that great event is well described in *King Cole* by Elizabeth Bonython, Victoria & Albert Museum, 1982, with excellent pen portraits of the principal personalities involved.

A full, illustrated account of the work of **Sir Joseph Bazalgette** in London and elsewhere is found in *The Great Stink of London: Sir Joseph Bazalgette and the Cleansing of the Victorian Metropolis*, by the present author, published by Sutton Publishing, 2001 (paperback, £9.99). The book is available direct from the publisher (£8.00 post & packing free). Contact Haynes Publishing, Sparkford, Yeovil, Somerset, BA22 7JJ; telephone orders 01963 442030; cheques or credit cards accepted. Quote ref. GS. An account of the development of the London Underground and the part played in it by **Sir Edward Watkin** may be found in *Underground to Everywhere*, also by the present author, Sutton Publishing, 2001, available from the same address. A full account of Watkin's career is to be found in *The Second Railway King: the Life and Times of Sir Edward Watkin*, by David Hodgkins, Merton Priory Press, 2001.

Two recent books are particularly recommended on **Alfred Waterhouse's** work at the Natural History Museum. These are *Alfred Waterhouse and the Natural History Museum* by Mark Girouard, Natural History Museum publications, 1999; and *The Natural History Museum at South Kensington, 1753–1980*, by W.T. Stearn, also published by the Natural History Museum, 1998. A broader consideration of Waterhouse's career is to be found in *Alfred Waterhouse, 1830–1905*, by Sally Maltby et al., published in 1983 to accompany an exhibition of Waterhouse's drawings at the Royal Institute of British Architects. It is available through good public libraries.

Index